# DISCOVER
# YOUR HIDDEN
# MEMORY &
# FIND THE
# REAL YOU

# DISCOVER YOUR HIDDEN MEMORY & FIND THE REAL YOU

## DR MENIS YOUSRY

This book is an exploration in human consciousness; how to change who we think we are and how to become who we really are

HAY HOUSE

Australia • Canada • Hong Kong • India
South Africa • United Kingdom • United States

**First published and distributed in the United Kingdom by:**
Hay House UK Ltd, Astley House, 33 Notting Hill Gate, London W11 3JQ.
Tel: +44 (0)20 3675 2450; Fax: +44 (0)20 3675 2451. www.hayhouse.co.uk

**Published and distributed in the United States of America by:**
Hay House, Inc., PO Box 5100, Carlsbad, CA 92018-5100.
Tel.: (1) 760 431 7695 or (800) 654 5126;
Fax: (1) 760 431 6948 or (800) 650 5115. www.hayhouse.com

**Published and distributed in Australia by:**
Hay House Australia Ltd, 18/36 Ralph St, Alexandria NSW 2015.
Tel.: (61) 2 9669 4299; Fax: (61) 2 9669 4144. www.hayhouse.com.au

**Published and distributed in the Republic of South Africa by:**
Hay House SA (Pty), Ltd, PO Box 990, Witkoppen 2068.
Tel./Fax: (27) 11 467 8904. www.hayhouse.co.za

**Published and distributed in India by:**
Hay House Publishers India, Muskaan Complex, Plot No.3, B-2, Vasant Kunj,
New Delhi – 110 070. Tel.: (91) 11 4176 1620; Fax: (91) 11 4176 1630.
www.hayhouse.co.in

**Distributed in Canada by:**
Raincoast, 9050 Shaughnessy St, Vancouver, BC V6P 6E5.
Tel.: (1) 604 323 7100; Fax: (1) 604 323 2600

© Menis Yousry, 2011

A catalogue record for this book is available from the British Library.

Every effort has been made to obtain permissions to print copyright
material. If any permissions have been missed, the publishers will be
pleased to include any necessary credits when the book is reprinted.

ISBN 978-1-84850-429-5

Printed and bound in Great Britain by
TJ International, Padstow, Cornwall.

TO MY CHILDREN, JAMES AND RUSSHA

# CONTENTS

# CONTENTS

# ACKNOWLEDGEMENTS

I would like to thank the following people for assisting me in the creation of this book:

Sukhy Loyal, Daphne Trotter, Natalia Nikolova, Milena Nenkova, Graham Edwards and Dr John Briffa.

To Naomi Fowler for her support and commitment in editing the book. To Ben Brophy who inspired me to write the book through his deep commitment to, and above all his love for, sharing wisdom and knowledge on a massive scale.

I would also like to thank the following people for supporting me over the years:

John Duggan, Jon Walsh, Terry Tillman, Mike Conner, Jacob Handelman, Desislava Dare, Poliksena Kostova, Jennifer Evans, Asia Dimitrova, Yvette Nagy, Sági Miklós, Dina Nikolits, Graham Edward, Judit Berki, Diana Karabinova, Will Skaskiw, Jean Crawford, Marian Ingleby, Zoltán Disznós, Adrian John Oliver, Dr Amal Treacher, Andy Metcalf, Dr Barry Mason, Delia and Simon Gray, Ely Varghai, Erika Balogh, Grant Stapleton, Isabel Losada, Linda Julian, Michael and Marcelle Lawson, Paul Higgs, Sam Westmacott, Sarah Brooking, Sarah Haigh, Siobhan Soraghan, Steve Nobel, Boriana Racheva, Rumyana Peneva, Fidanka Chingova, Ben Gabbitas, Peter Goryalov, Andy Morse, Delyan Zagaryov, Janet Parker, Graham Hadley, Merrel Gering, Leon Norell, Sir Ralph Halpern and Helen Harnden.

# PREFACE

## A journey into human consciousness

This book will take you on a journey of exploration into your consciousness and show you how it has been shaped by your early experiences of becoming conscious. Your consciousness is created even before you are born, as well as during your childhood, by your relationship with your parents, your origins, past generations, your culture and your environment. This is a journey about all the powerful, invisible waves of influence – positive and negative – that shape our lives, and how these combine to try to help us make sense of what we perceive ourselves to be as human beings. It is about how such experiences interweave and bind us to our past and to our present, thus creating our future.

Often these waves of influence generate hidden dynamics – made up of unresolved issues, beliefs, painful experiences and unusual circumstances – that we haven't fully understood in the past. These are stored in our subconscious memory and hidden from our conscious mind, and they affect our present perception of the world profoundly. These hidden dynamics are then repeatedly reinforced when we unconsciously attract matching life situations and circumstances into our lives.

The human consciousness is about completion. In our desire to complete and heal such incomplete painful past experiences, they become repeated patterns. They often keep manifesting themselves in our lives simply because we haven't yet made sense of them. They are unresolved patterns that keep recurring despite our attempts to find a solution and completion.

By exploring our hidden memories, we can explore how we can change who we think we are and become who we really are; in other words, we can learn to live consciously *now,* in our essence. It is a journey into your heart and soul to seek peace and find healing by exploring what it is to be human – as a child and an adult, within a family or culture. It is also a journey into what it means to be human in a world which we perceive to be part real, part illusory and within a universe of our own making.

Our compelling challenge is to explore our ability to uncover, expose and ultimately observe all these hidden dynamics within ourselves, our families and our cultures in order to reveal our internal model of reality and how, until now, we have perceived the world. Gaining this powerful understanding of ourselves will explain why we tend to gravitate towards either re-creating the same situations or trying and failing, repeatedly, in our attempts to create the opposite.

On the way to discovering your hidden memories, and ultimately yourself, we look at the patterns formed by the neurological connections in our brains as well as the way in which our origins and past generations bring us to an understanding of our culture and our place in the world. This knowledge will lead you to a greater awareness of yourself and your life and, in turn, will help you to eliminate further suffering and achieve future success. The key to this transformation is to find peace in understanding in our selves, as human beings in this unfolding universe.

Real freedom comes from within us and is not dependent on others. We can be set free from seeing ourselves as being merely a product of the past (and how this affects us in the here and now). People who are forever talking about seeking freedom are often trapped in the prison of their past and are trying to escape from something that actually no longer exists.

## Finding your hidden memory

The materials in this book come from a wide range of sources and developed from my interest and experience in the fields of human potential, social change, culture, psychology, art, psychotherapy, spirituality and academic research. Some of this information emerged during my research into memory, brain studies and biology. They are all essential disciplines that are relevant to understanding our hidden memories. The study of memory and the brain is extremely complex, however, so I have tried to keep the complex and overly technical biological information as straightforward as possible, as a full explanation of all the specific detail is beyond the scope of this book. When I mention the brain, or certain parts of the brain, you must bear in mind that there is a bigger picture that is constantly evolving concerning our knowledge of the brain, likened, for instance, to how computers are evolving technologically. In a few years' time we will know even more about the brain and how it affects our behaviour. A great deal of the other information in this book comes from my personal insights and through my work with people in therapeutic settings, in my Essence Foundation Courses and from the many people who have inspired my journey of self-understanding.

It is important that you shouldn't believe everything that you read in this book. By this I mean that it is important that you draw your own conclusions about what you read and that you trust your intuition *(in-tuition)* and your own teachings. You will automatically recognize what is true for you. Our knowledge is always limited because we are constantly evolving and this book offers you the means to explore inner healing and wisdom through your enhanced knowledge, reflection and insight, and offers ways of making changes in your life. What it does not offer is a *method* of any kind, other than that which works by looking deeply inside you. Many have tried using *methods* or *systems* to bring about changes in their lives but without success. Methods can distract us from the here and now. Since we are programmed to believe that we can ultimately solve all our problems by doing something about them, however, we find ourselves seeking out and hopping from one *formula*, *teacher* or *secret* to another. These methods of gaining self-understanding are inevitably short-term solutions and do not reach the depths of our being to effect lasting results.

This is not a self-help book or a replacement for your wisdom; it is a prompt and a reminder that you can live your daily life in, and from, your own awareness.

It is, in fact, a reminder of WHAT YOU ALREADY KNOW.

# PART I

# The Conflict Between Our Intentions and What We Achieve

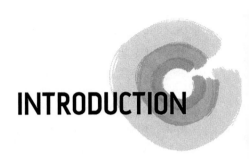

# INTRODUCTION

*The core of how we come to know ourselves hinges on the perfect dance between our deep inner world of feelings and our outer actions. The mysterious discord between these two worlds – our actions and how we intend to act – is interwoven with waves of inner processes that colour our emotions and affect our decision-making and actions; they can be the making or the breaking of us.*

## We are the reflections of our beliefs

Each one of us wants to have health, wealth, good relationships and happiness. Many teachers and books speak about our potential to achieve anything that we want in life. Even though we might believe them – consciously and intellectually – we can find ourselves disappointed to observe that we still don't get everything we want out of life and carry on struggling to achieve our dreams. It can be even more frustrating to observe that our communications, relationships and interactions with others do not match our honest intentions and what we deeply desire.

We have all experienced in our communications with people how, on many occasions, we do not say the things that we meant to say at the time. Later on, this can lead to self-doubt, as we realize that we were correct in our thoughts but were unable to act, even though we knew deep down what we really wanted to say or do.

How many times do we say to ourselves that we will never do something again but then we do it again? How many times do we explode or react adversely and then regret what we have said? Even if, at the time, we know that we aren't doing or saying the right thing, we go ahead and do it anyway. How many times have we ignored our inner voice? How many times have we reacted in a way that makes us dislike ourselves?

We could be forgiven for coming to the conclusion that we are made up of many parts; that is, there is a conflict between how we see the world and others, and our reactions to the experiences we face in everyday life with our relationships with people. Our responses to our experiences don't meet up to our personal reality. It is this mystery that discovering your hidden memories can help you to unfold.

## Our first programming

The first step is to begin to see that the programming we receive early on in our lives can hinder changes that we want to make later on. Often we can't understand why we are getting negative results and failing to fulfil our full potential. In addition, we may fall into the trap of blaming our lack of achievement on others, or put it down to bad luck or mere circumstances, without realizing that we are the creators of the results we achieve (or don't). The fact is that we actually sabotage ourselves due to our unconscious opposing beliefs that contradict what we really want.

Dwelling in our deep unconscious there is a weight of time and tradition urging us in a particular direction. The conscious mind may, to some extent, control and guide itself in the present, but in the unconscious mind our unsolved problems, compulsions, superstitions and fears are lying in wait, throbbing and urging, dictating our feelings and, therefore, our behaviour. These things can bring about the very opposite of our conscious desires and dreams.

This mystery lies in the unknown void between our actions and what we intend to do. The core of how we come to know ourselves hinges on the perfect dance between our deep inner world of feelings and our outer actions. The mysterious discord between these two worlds – our actions and what we intend to do – is interwoven with waves of inner processes that colour our emotions and affect our decision-making and actions; they can be the making or the breaking of us.

Our journey begins by making the connection between our thoughts and deep unconscious feelings. Our feelings are the main focus here because they are the energy that drives our behaviour. By exploring all these limitations we can discover how to create more effective ways of living and getting what we want out of life.

## The conflict between intention and action

Let us start by exploring when the conflict between our intentions and actions begins, using the notion of the conscious and the subconscious mind in relation to our experiences in life.

Our life is a reflection of our subconscious mind. By looking into this mirror we will see that the reason we cannot achieve the things we want is that we carry models and beliefs that our subconscious won't allow us to.

It is widely accepted that consciousness falls into two parts: first, our conscious mind now – we can call this our essence (which we could also call our heart or our inner voice, and this is who we are) – and second, our personality, which we use to present ourselves to the world. Many people think that personality is who they actually are but the challenge we face in life is that we are born into a family and carry our family's beliefs and culture, as well as the thoughts and feelings of past generations. Consequently, our personality has been developed and shaped by other people's lives as well as by our own life experiences, education, culture, parents and family. These two dimensions of our consciousness can be in conflict, as our intentions don't often conform to what is expected of us and how we *should* behave.

Even though we continue to learn and grow until the last day of our lives, it is widely accepted that most human conditioning, which makes us who we are, occurs during the early years of life. This conditioning can either help us to achieve or fail to reach our goals and dreams in adult life.

The first relationship you have is with your parents, in particular your mother, and this relationship forms the model for your relationships throughout the rest of your life. The mother represents the gateway for life; before we were born we experienced the mother's world and emotions. The very first moment the mother sees her child, she sets the tone of life for that child. The early bond between a mother and her child releases the mother's store of conscious and unconscious memory and the depths of her inner world. In this way, the mother shapes the structure of her child's social brain. The father too, by his attachment and interactions with his child, reveals his unconscious beliefs and values in the way he deals with and contributes to creating his child's reality. The parents' ability to be responsive and nurturing has an impact on the child's self-image and social interactions throughout the rest of his or her life.

## Our first training

In *The Secret Life of the Unborn Child*, Dr Thomas Verny MD, with John Kelly, explains that the womb is the first experience that we have of the world and it is the first home the unborn child experiences. If the womb environment is affected by emotions of anxiety or even rejection within the mother, then the child first experiences the world as an unfriendly place.

In cases where the mother wanted to have an abortion, has a conflict with her partner or experiences any other recurring difficult emotions during pregnancy, the child's *home* may feel unsafe. Even if, for example, the mother had an abortion on a previous occasion and is unable to rid herself of the guilt, then these feelings may also be transmitted to her unborn child. Past experiences that create a pattern of negative feelings about the pregnancy may also impact on her unborn child; just as the baby is constantly taking nutrients and oxygen from her blood, so the baby also feeds on her emotions.

Dr Dominick Purport, editor of the *Brain Research Journal*, supports this theory and states that awareness begins before we are born. Between 28 and 32 weeks, the brain circuit begins to form and the unborn baby can tune into the thoughts and dreams of the mother.

It is theorized that the mother's thoughts and feelings while pregnant can etch themselves so deeply on the child's psyche that they can remain throughout their lives. These feelings define and shape the child's emotional life and may create threats, which are engraved on the mind of the unborn child. It can take a great deal of work on oneself to change such effects.

Dr Verny theorizes that unborn children anticipate what the new world will be like based on their very first experiences. If the unborn child feels unsafe early in their development, then they establish unconscious expectations that the world is going to be the same as the one they experienced in the womb. The child is predisposed to a certain personality in the way they relate to others. Life on the outside can be much harder if our womb experience was not a friendly one.

The unborn child's emotional, intellectual and neuro-logical capacities aren't fully developed and so these experiences may be at feeling level only. While brain connections and circuits may not affect personality, they are extremely sensitive to malfunctions and inconsistencies. Dr Verny also states that feelings such as love and rejection affect the unborn from an early age. As the baby's brain matures, primitive sensations and feelings grow into more complex feelings, thought states and later into ideas.

If there are already inconsistencies in the mother's life, often they also continue after the birth and the baby is already predisposed to such vulnerabilities.

## Second stage training

From birth we are trained by other people (usually our parents) on how to live. They train us in the same way they themselves were trained, as they think it is the best way. This is because their aim is for us to survive in this world as best we can, according to the dictates of their conscious and subconscious (hidden) worlds. They train us about how to live and how to react and interact, so that our personality becomes a form of protection developed *outside* us in order to enable us to deal with the world. Our personality is therefore shaped by our perceptions and the reactions we accumulate, and develops from early childhood, as well as in response to our many experiences along the way. Thus, it is this part of us upon which our personal identity is constructed. Such a construct continues to be helped – and hindered – by the demands of others; for example, the people who bring us up and the society to which we belong. This same personality develops by attracting similar experiences that eventually reinforce the memories and beliefs that caused it to come into being in the first place.

Over the years, as this reactive dynamic grows and evolves beyond the original role of protecting us, we find that it has developed a life of its own. This kind of personality is actually a powerful network of unconscious attitudes and patterns of behaviour, which can dominate almost every aspect of our lives. The consequences, therefore, are behaviours that run contrary to who we really are and what our intentions are. This is especially true of intentions that are lodged deep in our essence (our subconscious) and which we keep on trying to carry out. In addition, it can often be the case that these behaviours actually have supported us in many ways and brought about a lot of our success in later life.

There is much pressure put upon us from the outside world, because those who raised us put pressure upon us in the same way as they experienced at the hands of their parents. In addition, we have become the same as them because we involuntarily copy them as a result of the training they have given us. This may cause a clash between our intention and what we achieve in life.

In order to resolve this clash we need greater understanding of the two parts of our consciousness – our subconscious and our conscious. The subconscious mind houses our powerful beliefs and perceptions. When we become adults, we function using basic assumptions and sets of reflex actions but we often are not able to identify them. These assumptions result from our experiences in our past and the influences of our parents, culture and religion. Of course, these assumptions have a huge impact on our lives. They are manifested every day in the ways that we react to each moment and event.

Such reactions are the main cause of the conflict between our intention, coming from the conscious mind, and our actions, originating from our subconscious mind. Our essence is our consciousness now. It is highly creative, evolving with life and creating endless dreams and aspirations. Whenever we lose our centre or focus, however, the conscious mind is hijacked by the subconscious. This produces reactions and results that contradict our conscious intentions. Because the majority of our consciousness is subconscious, that means we react unconsciously most of time.

So, how can we learn to live consciously?

# CHAPTER 1
# HOW OUR SOCIAL BRAIN MAKES US WHO WE THINK WE ARE

*Our social brain plays a crucial part in shaping our identity and how we define ourselves. The brain's constant rapid reactions to people and the environment form an image of who we are that may be very different from who we actually are.*

## Awareness and thought

We don't live in isolation. Our life and existence evolve from communication and other people. We live within multifaceted interconnections of social relationships, from the moment we are born until we die. The organization of the social brain is shaped, modified and built by all our interactions, relationships and communication with others and is, in particular, influenced by those who are most important in our lives. According to Dr Allan Schore, a leading researcher in the field of neuropsychology, 70 per cent of the brain is built after we are born, through our interactions and having to cope with changing experiences.

Our brain is in constant reaction to others but it is not in reaction to itself. In fact, it is the only part of our body that doesn't have any feelings or sensations. Ironically, it is aware of our sensations and feelings but does not *feel* anything itself. Its function is to remind the body of where pain and pleasure are; however, thoughts are manifested in the brain.

Do we have enough knowledge about the relationship between awareness and thoughts in the brain? Do we know how these thoughts arise in our consciousness? These are fundamental questions. Most research into the brain centres on its mechanics and how it affects our behaviour and bodily functions, but we have very little knowledge of how awareness creates our thoughts. There is something here that holds the secret of what it is to be human, both as decision-makers and in terms of who we are. We know the functions of every part of the brain – they are easily highlighted on brain scans – but we can't see the actual past, which dictates our thoughts, and how these experiences are then translated into awareness.

## The brain constructs its own reality

Grasping the connection between awareness, the workings of the human brain and relationships (its environment), will help us to understand how we manage to function in an inconsistent world.

We are surrounded by the mental world of others, just as we are surrounded by the physical world. The person with whom we are interacting in turn models most of our reactions and thinking. In return, this is how we experience ourselves in relation to others.

Our brain acts as an instrument for receiving, storing and communicating information, which is shared by us all. The energy emanating from our interactions is constantly being encoded in the brain, with the greater impact in our lives coming from parent–child interactions, which form the basic infrastructure of our experience of the world and of other people. Very often these experiences are reinforced and influenced by our early family relationships, such as the relationship between child and parents as well as other members of the family, and even with previous generations. We copy and learn everything from our parents. Every move they make, we notice. We learn from them by witnessing (perception) how they handle challenges and we could even go so far as to say that the unconscious parts of our parents' brains contribute to the organization of our own brain.

The brain constructs every experience and we call the result *reality*. Reality is the picture that we have built of the world in order that we might navigate our way through it. The brain constructs a model of reality and the more we map out this reality, the more we feel a sense of survival and safety. All our experiences shape and work through our brains in order to help us find the best way to survive. For example, any disturbance in the life of our family of origin can have a huge impact on how we react in our later life and relationships. The reactions that the brain learns can last for a lifetime.

The brain represents the boundaries between the world around and us. We are not separate from the world, we are part of it, and we share a field of information and energy that is not localized in the human brain. The brain receives signals and then absorbs the information, interprets it and gives us a model. Between the model and the real world are the brain's neuron activities. This is the reason why we sometimes experience the same situation differently at different times during our lifetime, because we have learned alternative ways of perceiving it and have consequently developed different beliefs – thus interpreting our reality in a different way.

## The conscious and the subconscious

It is also generally accepted that human consciousness consists of two parts: a conscious and a subconscious. The unconscious simply means what you are not conscious of. These two elements can be likened to the notion of short-term and long-term memory.

Neurobiologist Dr Bruce Lipton suggests that the subconscious mind stores information similarly to a recording device inasmuch as it records *programmes*. At the push of a button, it plays those programmes back to us and it will always play them back in exactly the same way. It is reasonable, therefore, to assume that this button is often triggered by stimuli from our environment. For example, if we are waiting for someone and they are late, it can trigger a *replay* of an earlier painful experience of abandonment. The trigger is therefore an emotional trace of a painful experience that is stored in the memory. Most people can't tell the difference between these programmes, as they are formed at a very early age (sometimes even during the last stages of foetal development). For example, the programmes stored in the foetus' subconscious mind were created through his or her experiences of the response of the mother and her environment.

Before a child is born and up to the age of five, the way a child observes and experiences the world is via programmes that are directly *downloading* information into the subconscious mind without any prior analysis or questioning. Repetition allows the information to go to our subconscious mind. This unquestioning download happens because the child isn't yet able to question or debate the accuracy of the information; they are simply just taking it all in. The huge amount of information that children receive comes from their parents, siblings and the community, and is downloaded into their subconscious minds as undisputed *truth*.

According to Dr Lipton, the conscious mind, the part that holds our conscious desires and aspirations for life, occupies a mere 5 per cent of the brain. The subconscious mind (containing programmes that we learned from our parents' and other people's beliefs) occupies the other 95 per cent of the brain. And it is the subconscious mind that is dominant most of the time.

This is a very important point in explaining why often, when we have determined to do something, we end up not achieving it; the beliefs in our subconscious mind are in direct contradiction to what we desire in our conscious mind. These subconscious beliefs override our conscious intentions because they are stronger and much more powerful.

## Our early programming

Even though humans become conscious three months before they are born, it is a consciousness of feeling and response. The higher neurological processing that leads to conscious discrimination of experiences does not manifest itself until we are around five or six years old. Therefore, a child is not really operating from a awareness of making sense of their experiences until after the age of five.

The first five years of our lives are a period of *programme installation*, upon which we draw later. As children, we download information from whatever we see, hear or experience from our parents and environment. This information is downloaded directly into our subconscious minds. Moreover, there is no conscious discrimination between the relative merits of these programmes. As children, we don't have the ability to debate whether the information is correct or not.

We learn how to become part of a family and wider community based upon these downloaded experiences. These programmes become lodged in our subconscious minds even though they may be falsehoods, because we aren't, as children, capable of reasoning, sifting through and questioning such information. In this way, it is easy for the subconscious to override our conscious mind and therefore our aspirations, desires and self-beliefs, thus affecting the outcome of our conscious efforts.

We can see that the subconscious mind contains programmes learned from others. We are *trained* in how to react to life. We *buy into* other people's beliefs and these run our reactions and communications most of the time. Such beliefs undermine and sabotage our natural abilities. In addition, they become limitations to our conscious desires to get things in life. The attitudes, perceptions and beliefs of the conscious mind are in direct opposition to the subconscious mind's programming. We play this programming in our conscious mind and yet, at the same time, we are not aware of it. We aren't aware that we are sabotaging ourselves repeatedly, and when we don't get what we want and desire out of life, we blame others, external forces.

Renowned scientist, scholar and author Gregg Braden suggests that each part of the brain works in a different way to make us who we are and to make our reality. The conscious mind is the one to which we are most connected and of which we are most aware. It creates the image we see of ourselves when we look from the inside out. It is the image of ourselves that we want other people to see.

The conscious brain takes on information about our day-to-day world, the people around us, the time of day, where we are going and how we plan to get there. The conscious mind analyzes and processes all of this information and then makes plans as to what to do once we get to where we are headed. When we find ourselves conforming or compromising, however, it is because our subconscious mind has made a different choice to our conscious mind. Unless we work hard on ourselves to recognize and identify this, we will be oblivious to the fact that there is a tug of war going on at all.

We may think we are choosing an action, but our brain has already made the choice without our conscious knowledge or *permission*. It means that we are not aware of having made that choice at an earlier time. Our experience of the time when that past action (and resulting choice) occurred does not bear a fixed relationship to our present. We don't see the object in front of our eyes until our brain has made inferences about what that object might be. In other words, we are not aware of the action we are about to perform until the brain has made a choice as to what that action should be. Our actions, in short, are determined by the choices we have made previously.

Gregg Braden also suggests that the subconscious mind can be likened to the brain's 'hard drive'. It contains a vast store of information and a record of everything that we have experienced in our lives. It is the place where our past memories reside. The perception we have of those past memories includes the functions that keep us alive and surviving each day. Most importantly, it holds a cross-referenced record of how we felt when processing each event while it was occurring, and this is the crucial reason why our present actions and reactions in life are affected by the past. Furthermore, this hard drive also stores every thought, emotion, criticism, betrayal and encouragement we have received. It is really important, therefore, to note that such a store of experiences can unexpectedly surface in our lives at moments when we least expect them and this can impact our lives in a negative way.

The subconscious mind never rests. Unremembered past experiences are still stored somewhere and can be activated at any time by a stimulus or trigger. Each day our responses are guided by the subconscious mind because it is larger and faster than the conscious mind. According to Dr Bruce Lipton, in his book the *Biology of Belief*, the subconscious mind can process 20,000,000 bits of information per second while the conscious mind can only process 40 bits per second.

This means that the subconscious mind has the capacity to process 500,000 times more information than the conscious mind. The power to move the world is therefore in the subconscious mind and it works instinctively, without the need for thought.

On the one hand, the subconscious mind can be very helpful and can save us a lot of trouble, for example in a dangerous situation, where it reacts rapidly and instinctively and does not analyze the situation before forcing us into action. If we were to wait for the conscious mind to save us, it might be too late.

For example, if a child is standing near the edge of a high cliff and hears his or her father shout the warning, 'Keep away from the edge – you could fall!', the child's subconscious mind absorbs this warning and realizes that in future it might not be such a good idea to stand near cliff edges, as it might result in a fall and subsequent death. They will not be using their conscious mind in the future to re-analyze whether it's safe to stand on the cliff edge; they just won't do it. On the other hand, we might pay a very high price for such fast responses when our reactions are based on the beliefs of others that we subconsciously learned to copy early in life.

> *'Could the young but realize how soon they will become mere walking bundles of habits.'*
> WILLIAM JAMES (1842–1910), AMERICAN PHILOSOPHER

All the information in our subconscious mind is made up of beliefs that were introduced when the brain was in a state of 'absorption'. According to Gregg Braden, this information was 'sold' to us when the brain was in a dream-like state and when it was like an absorbent sponge that soaked up information regarding the world around us, with no filters to tell us what was appropriate and what was not, what was right and what was wrong. The subconscious mind stored the information and it is only later that we discover whether this information is good or bad for us. The perfect example is being born into a family with a certain religion that we may defend or fight against for the rest of our lives.

# CHAPTER 2
# OUR BELIEFS ARE STRONGER THAN REALITY

*Our subconscious mind absorbs the way the people closest to us respond to their own life situations and we, by default, learn to emulate them.*

## The placebo effect

Human beings need beliefs to survive and my first introduction to this idea came when I was seven years old. My father was a pharmacist and, in Egypt in those days, many people used to go to the pharmacist for every illness, just like going to the doctor. My father was like a medicine man; he had a good reputation and was very popular. He always carried a little box in his pocket containing a few vitamin tablets and when people came to see him seeking his help (especially with psychological problems), he used to put his hand into his pocket, take out the little box and say, 'These are very special tablets and cost £1 each,' which was equivalent to £30 or more each in today's money but he only sold one or two at a time. The fascinating thing was that all of these people recovered very quickly. I asked my father why he was lying to people and he replied, 'If people think that this is the best and most expensive medicine, they will recover all by themselves.' He also added that healing was all in the mind and that if we believe that a medicine works, it will. I did not realize then that a placebo is in fact real medicine and I believe a time will come when what is known as the placebo effect will be the real medicine of the future.

There is a story about a man who had cancer and read in the paper about a new drug that claimed to heal people with his disease. He asked his doctor to prescribe it – the result was that he was healed from cancer. A few years later, however, he read in the same paper that, in fact, this drug had only a temporary effect. As a result, he developed cancer once more.

Family beliefs are also very powerful. For instance, there are families who often have the same type of diseases or other illnesses. In one case, two different families adopted one of a pair of twins, who had been separated at birth. One family had a history of cancer and, sure enough, the twin they adopted developed the disease. The other twin did not. Children brought up by divorced parents are more likely to divorce later on. Again, children brought up by poor parents are more likely to remain poor.

Beliefs are stronger than reality. You can see, from the above examples, how powerful beliefs can be. They can even change our reality so completely that they threaten our very survival and predispose our health, wealth and relationships in the future. At the same time, beliefs can heal us and allow us to survive better. This means that, in order to achieve anything we haven't experienced or achieved in the past, we must begin by changing our beliefs

*'The only difference between a sage or mystic
and ordinary, unenlightened man is that the one
realizes his identity with God or Brahman, whereas
the other does not.'*
ALAN WATTS (1915–73),
BRITISH PHILOSOPHER, WRITER AND SPEAKER

## The power of beliefs

In the same way, each culture has its unique beliefs and these have an impact on life, relationships and the way that people see and communicate with others from different cultures. Beliefs are a very important part of our consciousness and affect how we perceive life. The combination of the different ways in which the subconscious and conscious minds work together can make beliefs play a significant part in our lives. As you read this book now, the only difference between you and anyone else in your life is your beliefs. They are your theory of how the world works. Your beliefs originate from your parents' model of the world and they shape your interpretations and perceptions of reality.

Beliefs are derived from experiences that shaped our subconscious mind and are manifested without our conscious awareness. Beliefs shape our lives because our brain has an accurate record of every single thing and event to which we have ever been exposed. Our beliefs, therefore, are the foundation of what we hold to be true about the world at large and ourselves, and they take form in the very place where they were first created – in our minds. The brain creates our model of the world by prior knowledge but the clues to the origins of our beliefs are provided by our senses.

Our subconscious mind takes note and absorbs the way the people closest to us respond to their life situations and we, by default, learn to emulate them.

Beliefs are a way of feeling and absorbing experiences, so if our parents responded to the world in a psychologically healthy way, we benefit from their positive attitude and match their responses. Most of us learned our subconscious habits in an environment of mixed beliefs. Some are helpful and healthy beliefs and some are the opposite. This is why we often behave like our parents, because of the programming we received from them, and it can be very difficult to separate ourselves from them. It takes only a few hours for us to separate physically from our mother at birth, but a lifetime to separate emotionally.

According to Dr Lipton, we are often unaware of how our subconscious mind absorbed the beliefs of everyone around us, since we learned our own ways of living and behaving from our parents during the first five years of our lives, when we were simply taking in information. As mentioned earlier, Lipton defined this as the 'childhood download' period.

In many ways, we *are* our parents, because we carry them everywhere we go. Some parents find that their children display certain behaviours that they don't like about themselves. We are therefore also our children, because our children become like us. Observing them will teach us what we have carried on from our parents. The script is often faithfully followed. There are certain inner images and patterns we enact that were created from personal experiences and systemic connection with other family members. Such early memories are encoded into our being since our lives began.

We play out all these beliefs in our everyday life. Our world is a mirror in which these beliefs are enacted in the form of our relationships, career and choices, and even in our health. They manifest in the family and culture everywhere around us. And we also share collective subconscious beliefs in the wider field that surrounds us, which propels our relationship situations in real life. These beliefs are highlighted and brought more to the fore whenever we undergo changes and challenges in life; it is during these times that our deepest beliefs tend to surface in our relationships with others, where they can then be exposed. These times, therefore, offer us an opportunity to heal the negative beliefs about ourselves.

If we are not conscious of our beliefs, they can limit our achievements because we can't achieve anything while subconsciously contemplating the *impossibility* of achieving it. In this way some people live their lives trying to achieve their dreams and goals while at the same time spending most of the time subconsciously believing that they cannot get what they want. When they fail to get the results they want, they then spend most of their lives *consciously* believing that they cannot get what they want. This is because beliefs are the thoughts that we keep thinking, and we can therefore become what we think about because they are a reaction born from either the conscious or the unconscious.

The pattern of our beliefs reveals the interpretation and meanings we give to our experiences. These interpretations become integrated into the cells of our bodies and carry emotional energy, which affects our biography and, consequently, our biology. These interpretations become the lenses through which we see the world. When we seek something, we will find it.

Beliefs are crystallized in our nervous system and one way we often maintain our beliefs is by eliminating opposite beliefs. We do this in order to produce *evidence* or *proof* that we are right. For example, if you decide to buy a car of a certain colour and model, a few days before you buy it you may well notice this type of car everywhere. It is a trivial example but it shows how our beliefs can eliminate opposing ones. This is called *attention bias*, or selective attention. You have already eliminated all other cars from your perception because your focus is on this certain type of car. We eliminate other beliefs and focus on the belief we think about more. We do this is in many areas of our lives and we do it emotionally too; if we believe we are rejected, we may select and gravitate toward people who reject us. Such dynamics hurt us yet prove us right at the same time. So yes, we may be right, but we are right about being wrong *and* right at the cost of our own happiness and achieving our dreams. These are patterns we keep creating and they enforce our beliefs. The result is that we do not produce what we want, which strengthens our beliefs and consequently our beliefs get stronger and stronger all the time.

*'The deer hunter does not see the mountains.'*
ZEN PROVERB

## We are prisoners of our perceptions of the world

In some religions, people have a belief about the need to suffer. For example, they might believe that if they suffer long enough for something then it must be right. They justify suffering rather than admitting that it is time that they moved on to something else. There is also a belief that people who feel guilty are good people and guilt is one of the biggest obstacles that block our success. In some cultures, too, people are willing to kill each other and themselves for their beliefs.

With our beliefs in place, we will use all kinds of evidence for the sole purpose of supporting the position we favour. These beliefs thus become ideals and escape routes from facts. Beliefs and ideals can dissipate the energy that is needed to follow the unfolding of the fact – the *what is?* Beliefs are feeling the experience, and experience can shape not only whatever information enters our mind, but also the way in which the mind develops the ability to process that information.

Over the years we become attached to our beliefs and we argue with reality and often win, as we become very good at making up our own reality. While our beliefs can be stronger than reality, some part of us is still making choices based on meanings and constructed patterns that have grown out of past situations. We are attached to our beliefs because we feel lost without them; they are, in fact, our attempt to hang on to any kind of consistency in order to feel safe. It is very difficult, for instance, to go from being a socialist to not being a socialist, or to go from being religious to not being religious. When we feel under threat or unsafe, we often hang on to our beliefs even more, seeking security. This often happens with people who emigrate to other countries; they become much more attached to their culture of origin, traditions and religion in order to overcome the fear of isolation in the new culture.

*'My commitment is to truth, not to consistency.'*
MAHATMA GANDHI (1869–1948),
POLITICAL AND IDEOLOGICAL LEADER OF INDIA

Most of us are committed to something because we are attached to our beliefs. Beliefs about culture have divided humanity into Americans, Arabs, Russians, English, etc. Our beliefs, however, are always limited and create conflicts. The difference between those who are successful and those who fail is that the *failure* fails to recognize that he or she is successful. Because we are not conscious of our subconscious beliefs, we act them out even though they are obvious from the point of view of someone else. Just because we don't immediately identify our beliefs doesn't mean we will never know what these beliefs are and understand how they have an impact on our lives.

*'These then are my last words to you: be not afraid of life. Believe that life is worth living, and your belief will help create the fact.'*
WILLIAM JAMES

We live life with ideas that we are unable to dispute, as is illustrated by the story of the elephants in India. When the elephants are young, they are tied to a small tree so they can't escape. When they grow older they are prevented from escaping just by putting a rope around their leg, even though they could easily break free of their simple binds.

There is also a story about some travellers in the desert and their camels. They stop to rest for the night but find they are short of a rope to tie up one of the camels, so the owner pretends he is tying a rope around the camel's leg instead. Sure enough, the camel is fooled into thinking it can't escape. The following morning, as the travellers get ready to leave, the camel refuses to budge and its owner has to pretend to untie the rope before it will move.

In just this way, we are prisoners of our beliefs and we cannot escape because we do not know that we are prisoners in our own perceptions of reality. This can mean we are prisoners of our perceptions of the world. Our prison can become a comfort zone of which we are not aware. The question here is: how can prisoners create dreams outside their prisons?

According to *The Encyclopaedia Britannica*, the word 'belief' is described as 'A mental attitude of acceptance or assent toward a proposition without the full intellectual knowledge required to guarantee its truth.' According to this definition, there is no guarantee that beliefs reflect the truth. It is therefore fair to conclude that beliefs can actually filter our world and keep us locked into a limited vision of it that is almost a prison of our own creation.

## Exercise for the reader

*This exercise will help you to begin to uncover some of the beliefs you have. If you like, you can work through it with a friend, asking each other the questions and then seeing what the results are. When you reach the end, start again.*

- *Share something you want and don't have, for example a job, health, a relationship, money.*

- *What is stopping you from getting what you want? What are you doing to prevent yourself from having what you want?*

- *What are some of the beliefs that have stopped you from getting it?*

- *Where do these beliefs come from? Who else in your family has a similar belief?*

- *Can you think of an experience you've had that matches this belief?*

- *Is this belief true now?*

We actually respond to our perceptions of the world, not to external stimuli. Our perceptions are shaped by prior experience and re-shaped by matching experiences. In this way, our beliefs become stronger and stronger all the time. How we interpret the signals from our environment has a huge impact on our character. For instance, you can have two people walking down the street in the pouring rain and one person is upset because they are getting wet, while the other feels elated.

> *'We do not see the world as it is,*
> *we see the world as we are.'*
> THE TALMUD

Now we have established that our perception of the world puts us in a position that can limit our actions, we can also establish that if we change our perceptions, by examining our family and cultural beliefs, then we can change our perception of our world to create a new world in our minds.

*'If you change the way you look at things, what you look at changes.'*
DR WAYNE W. DYER, AMERICAN SELF-DEVELOPMENT
AUTHOR AND SPEAKER

# CHAPTER 3
# THE RELATIONSHIP BETWEEN BELIEF AND MEMORY

*Memory has painted many pictures of our lives on the canvas of our subconscious; they bind our lives together; the more we see them, the more they become who we think we are and they don't fade away with time.*

## Beliefs as memories

Our beliefs are memories formed from our past experiences, which have shaped us in our present. Beliefs also influence how we act, think and feel – not only today, but also into our future. Memory allows us to bring a reaction to an experience from one moment in time to another. Memory is not only intellectual recall, it is the mind's way of encoding information. We may not remember exactly everything that has happened to us in the past, but our previous experiences affect how we remember events and what we end up recalling from that memory. Therefore it is not memory that comes to mind when you want to remember something, it is the effect of it.

*What we are is what we think we are,
based on the way we react.*

The relationship between belief and memory is very relevant here. Memories are information resulting from what were once external experiences and were transformed into patterned neural activity distributed across many brain systems. We don't search our minds when we want to remember something. The past information in our subconscious seems to be contained in some form of memory, which then interplays with every other interaction we experience in life.

According to Joseph LeDoux, an American neuroscientist, our knowledge of who we are and the way we think about ourselves (and what others think of us), and also how we typically react to certain situations, is learned through experience. This information is accessible to us through our memory. This is how we can go back and forth, from who we were yesterday to who we want to become tomorrow. LeDoux also suggests that memory allows us to transport ourselves to an earlier time. We can go back a moment or most of our life. Memory is not perfect, certainly not literal; it is a reconstruction of facts and experiences, and it is a reconstruction by a brain that is different from the one that formed the memory in the first place.

*Everything in our lives fades except for our memories.*

## The unconscious mind and memory

The unconscious mind might be defined as the part of the mind that gives rise to a collection of mental phenomena of which the person is not aware at the time. These phenomena include unconscious feelings, unconscious or automatic skills, unnoticed perceptions, unconscious thoughts, unconscious habits and automatic reactions, as well as hidden phobias and concealed desires.

The conscious mind is the part of the mind that is responsible for logic and reasoning. It is the part that decides to take any voluntary action, such as walking or waving a hand. The subconscious mind is the part of your mind responsible for all of your involuntary actions, such as emotions, your heartbeat or your breathing rate. It is also the store of all your beliefs and memories.

The unconscious mind can be seen as the source of automatic thoughts (those thoughts that appear without apparent cause). It can be seen as the storehouse of memories that have been seemingly *forgotten,* or let us even say hidden, but which may nevertheless be accessible to our consciousness. It can also be seen as the place where the activity of implicit – we can call this hidden – knowledge is played out; that is, all the things we have learned so well that we do them without thinking about it, such as how to walk, how to brush our teeth, etc. A familiar example of the operation of the unconscious is the phenomenon where, for instance, you are facing a problem and can't find a solution but then wake up one morning with a new idea that resolves the problem.

It is presumed that when we are born we don't yet have memories but if there is a trauma in the mother's life, it can affect the baby's brain development in the womb and become a prenatal memory.

An individual in a family can begin to act in ways similar to a person who, say, was excluded, mistreated or had a difficult life. This is because we can inherit family patterns from previous generations. We may carry memories from our parents and these are transmitted to us even in the womb, as explained above. Even in cases of adoption or abandonment, there are still unbreakable connections to both biological parents. These invisible layers of our existence are hidden family connections and they can affect our lives and those of the next generation without us being aware of them.

We also carry highly subjective memories and internal images, which are personal snapshots of a hidden dynamic operating within a family. These images are, furthermore, influenced by the way a family copes with challenges and these continue to influence our actions and feelings in adult life.

Memory research is beyond the scope of this book but is, at the same time, crucial to understanding how we interact with beliefs and memory, and, more importantly, how they can rule our lives. Beliefs is another area of research that is extremely relevant to our purposes of understanding ourselves, as well as 'attachment research' pertaining to the relationship between parent and child. The following brief summary explains the role played by conscious and subconscious memories, which are very much influenced by our attachment to our parents and which, in turn, heavily influence our ideas and reflections about the relevance of our hidden memories in our current lives.

## Layers of memory

Memory can be divided into two main components: a conscious and an unconscious memory. It is important to think of memory as an associative process – that is, things that happen simultaneously, which then become linked to each other instantaneously. For instance, if a dog bites me repeatedly and I feel pain, the next time I see a dog I will remember that pain again and, perhaps, be afraid of dogs. Another example is a child who is told off for not being *good* when they are ill, when they become ill as an adult they won't feel *good* about themselves and therefore won't ask for help.

This means that if a stimulus that results in an emotional response (the fear of being bitten by a dog) is repeated together with another stimulus that does not cause an emotional response (seeing a dog), eventually the second stimulus will result in the same emotional response as the first. This is called 'learning by association'. This phenomenon was discovered by Ivan Pavlov, a twentieth-century Russian physiologist, and it is known as 'classical conditioning'. Pavlov presented meat to his dogs and combined this with ringing a bell. After the meat and bell were presented together several times, the bell was rung (auditory stimulus) and no meat was given. The dogs salivated nevertheless, purely in response to the bell.

While the bell began as a neutral stimulus (i.e. the bell itself did not cause the dogs to salivate), by pairing the bell with the stimulus that produced the salivation response (i.e. the meat), the ringing bell eventually triggered the same response on its own. Pavlov therefore demonstrated how stimulus–response bonds are formed and these form our basic building blocks of learning. Old associative learned situations are memories that are hidden in the unconscious mind and may be prompted into action by triggering events, such as seeing a fight or someone being punished. Such events can generate intense feelings of fear provoked by memories hiding in the deepest recesses of our subconscious mind.

According to Dr Daniel J. Siegel, known for his work on interpersonal neurobiology, there are two layers of memory. The first layer is called implicit or hidden memory and the second layer is called explicit memory.

## Implicit or hidden memory

Hidden memory is made up of unconscious patterns of learning in the unconscious layers of connections in the brain; these patterns are not accessible to our conscious awareness. We don't remember, in short, when we *learned* this memory. Sometimes it may even have been laid down before birth. This memory can only be triggered by associations between an event in the present and the original experience that created the memory.

Hidden memories can be expressed in the following ways:

*Emotions* – how we feel (fear, happiness, surprise, shame, disgust, etc.)

*Perceptions* – seeing a stimulus (visual association)

*Physical reactions* – motor behaviours or actions we perform (what we do)

*Body-memory sensations* – physical pain (experienced in the gut, the limbs, etc.).

For example, if we had a painful experience in the past, such as being attacked by a person or an animal, we will have experienced the emotion of fear. When a similar memory is triggered later in life, we will experience the same physical sensations in the body. In our hidden memory, however, there is no conscious awareness in the act of recollection. There is no involvement at all of the part of the brain called the hippocampus, because this part of the brain does not develop until the age of two.

Such reactions can also occur later in life as the result of traumatic events. The memory is concealed deep in our unconscious and hidden, and the consequences are flashbacks. This is where a person relives an experience from the past, as if it were happening in the present time. In wars or cases of rape and other intense traumatic events, the old experience can be relived in the present when provoked by stimuli in the environment that has an association to the past event that caused the painful experience.

For example, a woman who was raped by a father or a teacher may have this type of reaction if she sees someone similar to the person who raped her in a position of authority. Dr Bruce Lipton believes that the majority of our perceptions come from experience, particularly when patterns of behaviour are repeated. He uses the example of learning to walk; once we learn to walk we are no longer conscious of walking. After sufficient repetition, the information is in the subconscious mind and is 'programmed' within us. This programming can be anything from a damaging behaviour to a positive behaviour because the subconscious mind does not recognize the difference between good or bad, or positive or negative.

When a stimulus provokes a reaction in us, the subconscious mind is activated like a tape recorder and we play back the behaviour. Dr Lipton calls this a self-operating mechanism, once we are programmed. The stimulus response mechanism is a very powerful thing inside us and occupies a large amount of our consciousness.

According to Dr Siegel, traumatic experiences that occur before a child is 18 months old are not processed by the hippocampus and therefore the memories become hidden. Hidden memories can also be formed in adult life, as a result of a severe traumatic experience or taking drugs. The memory of those types of experiences won't be processed by the hippocampus. In other words, the memories are not put in the past and so they remain in the present. As a result, we get flashbacks and later fight-or-flight, or fight-or-freeze, responses when this memory is triggered.

Most brain researchers, such as Dr Siegel and Joseph LeDoux, suggest that the emotional-perceptual memory is retained in the form of hidden memory (memory never processed through the hippocampus). When this memory is retrieved we aren't aware that it is coming from our past. Like the sound of the bell in Pavlov's experiments, the event from the past (emotions, perceptions, bodily actions) will bombard us while we are absorbed in the here and now, and we won't realize that these feelings come from our past. These reactions are extremely vital to explore as they take control of us immediately and it is like being hijacked. It may appear that we are losing control and often regret our actions and are afflicted with the consequences.

For example, one of my clients suffers severe reactions when he has to travel on trains. We explored his fears and discovered that when he was young, his mother had a painful and traumatic experience on a train while he was with her. This type of experience can be a common cause of fearing of flying, too.

Another young man came to me for therapy due to his severe reaction toward using inhalers. We found out that when he was very young, he had a bad experience at the dentist's when they had tried to give him anaesthesia.

The above illustrations are of traumas and hidden memories that keep manifesting themselves in the present when similar stimuli are presented. It is crucial here to emphasize the meaning of hidden memory, because *here truly rests the secret of our conflicts in our daily lives.* Hidden memory simply means remembering something without being aware that we are remembering it. It is an unconscious form of memory, containing feelings, perceptions and reactions, which developed before we were able to understand them. These unconscious memories have a huge effect on our conscious experience.

In his fascinating work, Dr Wilder G. Penfield, one of the world's leading neuroscientists, demonstrated that when he operated on conscious patients, he was able to stimulate different parts of the brain. Consequently, the patients were able to emotionally re-experience past forgotten events and feel the emotions produced by such events. These events are always there in our hidden memories and they still have emotional resonances that can influence us in the present. This makes me wonder whether life situations can provoke us or stimulate us in similar ways. These life situations trigger reactions to past hidden events that are only forgotten by the conscious mind, not by the subconscious mind. Even though the experience is over and in the past, it can feel just as real because there is no sense of time with such memories.

As you can see, hidden memories can affect our thoughts without our conscious knowledge because they are experiences that have been transformed into neural connections and which don't age as the years go by. They remain in their initial form because they haven't been processed by the hippocampus.

## The priming effects of memories are often not conscious

The hidden memories are layers of emotions, sensations and physical actions, as well as mental models and *priming*. Priming means that an exposure to a stimulus can influence our response to a subsequent stimulus and this can occur following a repetition of a past event.

For example, if you are exposed to the word 'car' many times and see lots of photos of cars and later are asked to complete a word starting with 'ca', you are more likely to answer 'car' because you were primed. Even a little exposure to certain situations can increase the threshold in our subconscious, preparing us to react faster to such events. This is called 'unconscious priming' and its effects can be significant and long lasting, even more so than simple memory recognition.

Exposure to past events is an unconscious priming process and is usually formed early in life, present at birth or even before birth memory has been laid down. The simplest example is our experience of the world even before we are born because the mother's womb is an environment constructed by the mother's experience of the world. If her experience toward the pregnancy is consistently negative, we can be primed or predisposed to feeling negative emotions, too.

In the same way, if in our first few years we live in a negative environment, we can be primed and ready to take on more negative experiences than positive ones in later life. This can be at the root of how we limit ourselves in our day-to-day interactions and relationships.

Past unexplained painful experiences have produced activation patterns in the brain and become associated with each other. Even years later, they not only produce beliefs about ourselves, but also 'priming' effects to enhance our expectations before we approach stimuli in our environment. Dr Siegel also suggests that implicit (hidden) memory has a priming effect on the nervous system. This means that we can become afraid and get ready to predict a certain response in a certain way, even before the stimuli occur. These are very subtle layers of hidden memory; it is a fear-expectation of what is going to happen before it actually happens. This can be compared to a phobia, because we are already primed without heed to what has happened to us in the past and because we anticipate our reactions.

> 'All emotional conflicts grow out of memories.
> Whether the recollection is conscious ones or,
> as is more often the case, unconscious.'
> DR THOMAS VERNY MD WITH JOHN KELLY,
> THE SECRET LIFE OF THE UNBORN CHILD

# Explicit conscious memories

Explicit memories are the result of conscious learning of any kind, like play, language, smell, etc. This consists of memories from events that have occurred in the external world at a specific time and place.

Explicit memories can be remembered and recalled and rely upon previous experiences and knowledge because they are processed by the hippocampus. This part of the brain's main task is to encode the storage of explicit memory. It helps us to compare different memories and come to conclusions based upon previous learning. Dr Siegel's research shows that the hippocampus is the part of the brain that processes memories and turns them into what is called 'autobiographical memory' (as in 'this event' happened to me 'then'). In this kind of memory there is conscious recollection. The hippocampus helps the brain to makes sense of an experience and we know that the experience ended in time.

According to Larry R. Squire, Professor of Psychiatry, Neurosciences and Psychology, damage or blockage of the hippocampus can halt any new learning from occurring, making us forget anything we learn the second after we have experienced it. This comment by Squire is extremely relevant to understanding how our memory and beliefs affect our everyday life. It is important to talk more about this part of the brain as it explains how we make sense of our world.

After the age of two, explicit memories develop into factual memories. In addition, autobiographical memory, which develops after this age, carries with it internal sensations that we are recalling from the past. Autobiographical memory is constructive and re-constructed as an evolving process of history. A person's autobiographical memory is reliable and is a personal representation of general and specific events, as well as actual facts. Autobiographical memory also refers to the memory of a person's history.

Our autobiographical memory is reliable, although our perceptions of the memory can be questioned. These memories differ in special periods of life. People recall few personal events from the first years of their lives.

For example, if we don't make sense of our experience in the first years of life, we may presume that whatever happened becomes our fault because, at that time, we have no other frame of reference to process and understand things. For example, if a child is left alone for a long time when they are young, playing alone with very little support or parental stimulation, the child doesn't understand that the parents aren't able to be with them and may presume that it is their fault or that they have to find their own entertainment and occupy their time. It is often the case that these children grow up believing that people don't want to be with them and that if people do want to be with them, they have to do something or give something to them.

## The brain doesn't forget the past

What is fascinating about how the brain stores memory is that the memory is stored in a way that is never approximate. The brain has a perfect and exact recording of information; it keeps our history safely hidden and also keeps reminding us of our strengths and limitations. It is like someone who keeps telling us and reminding us of the truth, even when we don't want to hear it. It isn't the same as when other people keep telling us how good we are or when we read a self-help book that tells us how strong we are. Our brain, through memory, is very quietly reminding us of how we were ignored, mistreated and unloved, and to what extent we felt unimportant and unworthy. This was the reality that was imposed upon us at a vulnerable time in our lives. It is in the past, but the brain never forgets.

*'No one confines his unhappiness to the present.'*
SENECA (*c*.1 BC–AD 65), ROMAN PHILOSOPHER,
STATESMAN AND PLAYWRIGHT

Because our brains are designed to anticipate, assess, judge and react to every situation in the present, our reactions are usually based on past rather than present information. We can become almost paralyzed and unable to make sense of the experiences. After behaving in a way that is opposite to our intentions, we might, especially when we have had a chance to reflect on the experience with our conscious mind, ask ourselves why we keep repeating this behaviour. We can't question ourselves during the event because we aren't conscious of it happening; it is as if we are on autopilot and using out-of-date software, which is not supportive to the new situation. We can actually hurt others and ourselves this way, without realizing what we are doing; for example, by compulsive decision-taking and reactions toward others, or being quick to anger and even making the wrong assumptions and misunderstanding people. Alternatively, we may respond by compromising and withdrawing from situations that we should confront.

## Hidden memory: beliefs that are stronger than reality

We are deeply influenced by all our past memories, whether we are consciously aware of them or not. This explains why we possess certain prejudices and biases, even though rationally we think they are false. This is also why we can fight for our beliefs to the death, as if they were not just our beliefs, but also some kind of independent truth outside of ourselves.

> *'All of us have lost memories that from their hiding place – the unconscious – can exert a powerful influence over our lives.'*
> Dr Thomas Verny MD with John Kelly
> *The Secret Life of the Unborn Child*

Painful experiences derived from trauma or neglect, usually by our parents or family guardians, in our lives form our implicit (hidden) memories in the first few years of life. Children can't make sense of them because their brains aren't fully developed yet and they have no sense of self or time. The brain doesn't know that these memories come from the past, and when a memory emerges into the present, it can feel as if we are reliving an event from the past rather than simply retrieving a memory. These early memories can form powerful beliefs in our present and thus it is extremely difficult not to believe them.

## Dissociation

One of the ways we use to help ourselves survive painful experiences or memories is by a process called dissociation, which allows us to focus our awareness away from the traumatic event, such as a car accident or war trauma. Blood doesn't flow to the hippocampus so this doesn't engage or pay attention to the memory and we act as if nothing has happened to protect ourselves from the shock or emotions associated with the memory. Dissociation is an incomplete conscious processing and therefore the event stays, at an unconscious level, ever present.

This automatic mechanism for protecting ourselves is similar to the one the brain uses to improve the speed of our reactions when under present threat, for instance, from an oncoming car or being chased by a wild animal. If we are exposed to a very fearful or dangerous situation, all our resources will aim at survival, at producing the fight-or-flight response. In response to the danger, all the energy of the body and brain focuses on protecting ourselves and preparing the body to physically flee the danger and so no blood flows to the hippocampus. Our means of surviving painful memories, therefore, is by dissociation, in order to protect ourselves from severe pain.

In dissociation our awareness is turned away from traumatic events so that we avoid being engaged or remembering an event that is intensely painful or distressful to us. This often happens in the case of a severe accident where the injured person disassociates from feelings of pain. In order to dissociate from the memory, the amygdala, another part of the brain, helps the hippocampus to 'switch' off and focus on something other than the experience of pain, so we won't be aware of it.

According to neuroscientists Heather Berlin and Christof Koch, dissociative identity disorder is often associated with childhood trauma, such as neglect, or emotional or sexual abuse. It is a way of coping with an overwhelming situation, which is too painful or violent to assimilate into one's conscious self. The person just *goes away* into his or her head to flee from the anxiety-producing experience from which there is no physical escape. This process of dissociation allows traumatic feelings and memories to be psychologically separated, so that the person can function as if the trauma had never occurred.

Berlin and Koch state that the brain can generate two or more distinct states of self-awareness, each with its own unique pattern of seeing, thinking, behaving and remembering. This, therefore, divides our attention and disassociates us from the source of the trauma, thus protecting us from feeling the pain. The body focuses its energy on the adrenalin glands for fight-or-flight and the hippocampus is not engaged.

The fight-or-flight response is used to escape from the source of the threat. The muscles prepare for this escape by increasing their tension level; the heart rate and respiration increase and the metabolic system is flooded with adrenaline. Blood is diverted to the muscles, away from the internal organs, and we attempt to run away. If we can't escape, however, or we think we have a chance and the threat is not very strong, then we'll fight back. According to Peter Levine, an American psychologist specializing in trauma, if we have no hope of survival at all, we go into shock or a state of immobility; we can also enter a state of fear that is preparation for rage or a counter-attack.

Some research has also shown that adrenalin also has an effect on the hippocampus activity; this then becomes a memory. The more we see the memories, the more they become who we think we are and become encoded without our conscious awareness. Subsequently, the painful experience becomes part of our behaviour and physical reactions, and we may even develop mental models of how we see the world based on the experience. In the case of difficult family situations, we may carry models of violent relationships with us to old age and these deeply engrained memories can affect our behaviour and relationships with our partners.

When we dissociate from painful experiences, we deliberately avoid engaging our conscious mind; however, the hidden memory still formulates what happened by neuron-firing patterns, even if we have no conscious memory of them.

## Adaptation to stress

I have a client whose life has been one disaster after another. First, she experienced problems with her family and then her husband went to prison. She campaigned to have him released, then rescued one of her nephews from abuse and fought with the authorities to seek asylum for him. Afterwards, she moved to different countries and, each time she did so, she suffered huge amounts of stress from all the moving around. Her life seemed to be organized by very stressful events. In one of our sessions I asked her if there had been any time in her life when she hadn't had any problems at all, because I was trying to find some intervention for her to be able to imagine her life without stress. She told me that the summer of the previous year she'd had two months without any problems. I asked her what she had done then and she replied, 'I couldn't live with myself. I was very anxious.'

Her response had a huge impact upon me. Since childhood, this woman's life had been full of violence and abuse; her brain had been shaped by all the stress she had experienced and adapted in order to manage her difficulties. In addition, living a stress-filled life was the reality with which she was most familiar and, although she was often desirous of not having stress in her life, she needed a crisis with which to deal.

I am sure you can think of someone who has suffered one crisis after another and almost seems to thrive on them, and we often hear people say, 'It could only happen to me.' Often these types of people feel so calm in stressful situations that they create chaos in their lives in order to feel relaxed. Stress can become like an addiction, what the brain uses for stimulation, even though the person affected claims to prefer a peaceful life. We can see this in children who were brought up by chaotic or alcoholic parents; they, too, can become alcoholics because their brain has adapted to the stress of alcoholism and they need to stay in this familiar – and even, for them, in some ways comfortable – zone.

Dissociation, in the case of a traumatic experience, is laid down amid our divided attention. It is an adaptation by our mind so that we aren't overwhelmed by our past experiences. At the time of terrifying events we don't process events with the hippocampus, but our hidden memories can flood us later on in our relationships, behaviour, physical reactions and/or any emotions associated with the negative experience. This mechanism for protecting ourselves puts us at risk of reacting in chaos, for example fight (exploding), flight (running away) or shutting down (freezing).

The author Madhusree Mukerjee, in her research into childhood sexual abuse, found that children who suffer from long-term disturbances of the psyche with nightmares and flashbacks are psychologically similar to war survivors. Some display opposite feelings to fight-or-flight and may freeze and be calm in situations of extreme stress. Her research showed that survivors of child abuse might also have a smaller hippocampus due to hormones, which flood the brain during and after a stressful episode. She stated that between 10 and 20 per cent of adult survivors of child sex abuse are believed to suffer from dissociate disorders or post-traumatic stress disorder.

Children who can't escape from the threat of abuse often employ such dissociation. The means of mentally withdrawing from a horrific situation separates it from conscious awareness and allows the victim to feel detached from the body or *self*, as if what is happening is not actually happening to them. People suffering with post-traumatic stress disorder tend to relive violent memories, especially when they see or imagine a similar stressful situation or, for instance, when they are in the presence of someone who is threatening. They are easily distressed, avoid clues that remind them of the original experience and become intensely agitated when confronted with such stimuli.

The brain's function and ultimate aim is to support survival and procreation, and so it is important to understand how the brain copes with memories and the impact they can have on our consciousness that lead to an altered sense of self.

Dissociation is the body's natural coping mechanism and it is designed to help us deal with intense pain. Don't be alarmed by these brain studies and think that if you have suffered trauma there is something wrong with your brain. Our understanding of how the brain works is extremely limited but gaining insight into how these coping mechanisms affect our later lives is often the first step in transforming your reactions after a painful childhood experience. It is clear so far that the beliefs have been formed from past experiences. These experiences have lived in us as hidden and unhidden memories, and therefore memory is the real focus because it is in understanding memories that we can unfold the mystery of how and why we re-act out our past experiences in the present.

## The memory we remember and the memory we don't

The hippocampus organizes experience into a person's view of the world. If the brain processes an experience (makes sense of the experience), then it is completed in our consciousness and we can reflect on what happened and deal with it. This is a memory we can remember. If, however, the brain doesn't process the experience, then it turns into an unresolved memory.

Such psychological emotional reactions or disturbances remain unresolved in the system and are incomplete, and consequently the brain is more likely to try to keep going back to them in an attempt to resolve these experiences. All these reactions are formed unconsciously in the brain in the form of memories that we don't remember.

This is why we often recall more negative childhood experiences than positive ones. The former are unresolved memories, which have not been completed because we were too young and inexperienced to make sense of them. Consequently, our response to any new similar experience is conditioned by the unresolved past reactions and is always protective. Because all new experiences are dealt with in a limited way, we create very interesting patterns generally based on past repeated and unresolved matters. Such generalizations form a wide range of presumptions that then shape our perceptions.

*We are more likely to recall more negative experiences than positive ones because we have not been able to make sense of negative events and accept them. They are therefore unfinished and what is unfinished is remembered in order to be finished.*

Because the brain learns many things, which function outside of conscious awareness, we find that we actually begin to relate to these reactions as being part of *who we are*. Understanding this point is the key to understanding ourselves as we begin to see the relationship between our memory and our emotions. This is particularly true of reactions to pain and/or fear and so it is worthwhile being more aware of how specific events or stimuli, arrived at through individual learning experiences, provoke a particular manner or behaviour in us. And to understand also the way the brain shapes how we deal with significant and emotional events and what happens to our emotional memory.

## Memories of pain and fear

In order to survive, we are born with the capacity to be afraid, as a means of avoiding threatening situations. According to Joseph LeDoux, the amygdala is the part of the brain that controls fear. It is able to detect whether danger exists and, thereafter, what amount of fear we must use in order to protect and aid ourselves. You can see this in all animals; they are very sensitive to danger and fear is their survival mechanism. The main function of fear is to protect us from danger.

The amygdala sends a message to other parts of the brain, which then trigger the adrenal glands in order to increase the amount of muscle energy for the purpose of running away (flight approach) or confronting (fight). Some studies have also shown that stress hormones divert blood glucose to supply the muscles with energy so we can fight or take flight in the face of danger. The amount of glucose (energy) that reaches the brain's hippocampus is therefore diminished. This then creates an energy crisis in the hippocampus, which compromises its ability to process memories and make sense of experience and time.

The main purpose of the fight-or-flight response is to help us to survive – the ultimate goal for human beings. According to LeDoux, a neuroscientist, the Henry and Lucy Moses Professor of Science, and professor of neuroscience and psychology at New York University, the system involves transmission of information about the outside world to the amygdala, which then controls our response and forms the most appropriate reaction. If the amygdala detects danger, then it engages with the response to it. This is a natural response for our protection.

For example, a child in a dangerous situation does not have the intellectual ability that an adult possesses to deal with the experience. While they may not survive the painful experience without this protective response, unfortunately such responses become hidden memories that feed our learning and are then used again when we are adults. We do not know when we are creating helpful and unhelpful memories.

We are designed not to have this ability at an early age in order to survive. This is why in deep traumatic situations we no longer process the information with our intellect or via the hippocampus.

The problematic consequence of this is that the memory of danger then actually stays unrecognized and becomes hidden memory. To clarify, if an event occurs that has an element of danger or threat and the child does not deal with it as an adult would do, and does not understand the consequences of these experiences on his or her wellbeing, then this is a memory that is not quite processed or organized; it is not put into the past as something that is complete, for example an hidden memory. It is like a predisposition to danger that we don't understand; the early experience can go back as far as the stressful experience in the womb.

Stressful events can paralyze the brain's organization of memory and turn it into hidden memory. Consequently, such memories continue to be alive and reverberate in the system, unconsciously seeking resolutions. The impact upon our lives is therefore tremendous.

We can see how stressful situations, such as lack of love or care, hurt, abuse, rejection, early experience of parental rejection, criticism or neglect, are very stressful to children and fear is the only protection they have to survive the experience. We aren't conscious of processing the painful event because the brain's total attention is focused on surviving in order to protect us from danger. The child doesn't have the ability to make sense of the painful experiences or to justify why he or she is being treated in this way, especially if the painful treatment comes from the people who are most important to him or her. The unbearable pain of the experience is what the child is left with.

> *'Psychoanalysis shows that the human infant,*
> *as a passive recipient of love, is unable to*
> *bear hostility.'*
> KARL STERN (1906–75), GERMAN–CANADIAN
> NEUROLOGIST AND PSYCHOLOGIST

## The social brain

In a report in the 14 October 2003 issue of the journal *Biological Mind*, Randall Parker stated that humans are wired not to want to be rejected by other humans, while researchers at UCLA have demonstrated with MRI scans that the pain of rejection looks similar in a brain scan to the neural activation pattern seen in physical pain.

This research indicates that the only way for the child to survive pain is by reacting with fear. This reaction is very important because it helps the child to survive and creates further brain connections by the transmission of information (neuron connections). These connections are retained in the hidden memory, in which past experiences and adaptations (fear responses) are generated in response to danger.

The brain creates neurological connection-reactions from the fear experience. As long as the memories of the painful feelings exist, the fear remains as a reaction, and as a memory too.

Painful experiences are not only what we experience in our family or as a result of what happened to us in childhood. Early separation from our main caregiver, usually the mother, is also a painful experience. Attachment to the mother symbolizes survival and so being cut off from the mother can cause pain to the child. This reaction has been shown by research on monkeys; those that are separated from their mother have a lower chance of survival.

Our brain functions in relation to other people and we can't exist alone. The brain is structured to connect and interact with others. Separation can be extremely painful for us. Our relationship with a significant other is so important in helping to shape our neurophysiology that it has an impact on our social and emotional development. The structure and function of the brain and the development of the nervous system are determined, shaped and modified by experiences that are primarily social in nature.

A child who has been abused by a parent will find this an extremely difficult and complex situation to understand. The child wants and expects the parent to be a source of comfort and love, instead of which the child receives emotional and physical abuse (and in extreme cases, sexual abuse). These children can adapt to this difficult situation so that they will still love the abuser and hate him or her as well. This can be transferred to their personal relationships in adult life.

Losing the love from a caregiver (or from other people close to them in their early years) can have a devastating effect on a child and last a lifetime. This can be manifested in the early interaction between mother and child or in the absence of significant others in the child's world.

It is important to clarify that children don't understand what love is but feel it in their soul and suffer the absence of love by how their parent or parents react. This is really the core of the pain that many of us face in life, and the consequences are tremendous, lasting throughout our lives and into old age. I will go further and say that this abandonment affects our children and our grandchildren, too, as well as all our relationships in life, because they also are exposed to the pain that is in our hidden memories.

## The search for love

Each child wants to receive love and closeness from his or her parents and any disturbance crucially affects the rest of his or her life. The sudden deprivation or withdrawal of love has an effect on the child's brain. After all, the child was in a state of unconditional love before birth as the mother provided everything and so when there is a change after birth and they no longer receive this loving nurture, it has a devastating effect. The parents themselves might not have had all the love and care they also needed, or other circumstances might have stopped them from providing their child with love. We can't give what we don't have.

The lack of love and the consequences this has upon our lives is an issue in child development, which has been explored and researched in psychology for many years. The best-known research concerns attachment theories, which explore the relationship between mother and child. The search for love is the most fundamental need that humans possess.

I need to emphasize here that love has an effect on our brain function and how we manage in the world because the brain is the link between the world of relationships and us. Whenever I mention painful early experiences, I am really talking about the deprivation of love. Early painful experiences become the foundation from which all other experiences derive, and they attract more reminders and require more effort in our search for consolidation and resolution of them. These are all the experiences that we haven't understood and they produce so much fear that they can affect everything we do throughout our lifespan. This particularly applies if the mother has not stimulated a child and has not transferred security to him or her, thus enabling the child to cope with the ever-changing energy of his or her environments.

We do not understand all this when we are young. Our brain's job is to help us survive, yet it has recorded the painful memories in a false attempt to protect us the best way it can. The brain is designed to cope with the constant changes in an unsettling world of relationships through amazing adaptations to changes in our environment that are essential to our survival. Such adaptations were helpful at a certain time in our lives. But not later on in life when we have developed our intellect which allows us to cope. At these later times such adaptations actually paralyze us.

## The relationship between pain and fear

The relationship between pain and fear is very important and relevant to our behaviour and our decision-making in life. If the pain of an early experience is intense, fear becomes stronger and acts as an agent of survival. It keeps the child alive by not allowing his or her to feel the shattering painful feelings that may cause his or her destruction. It also allows us to block the feeling of pain and, even later on in our adult life, keeps us from feeling the hurt.

Fears are also hidden memories and are unpleasant and painful. We don't want to feel fear; we avoid it at all costs and try to suppress it the same way that fear suppresses pain. Fear then leads the child into producing coping personality reactions to protect him or her from the unpleasant pain and, later, fear, which is perceived as a threat or disaster. Such protective reactions also become hidden memories in the form of emotional, physical and visual reactions to stimuli. The child begins to put up a character front as a defence mechanism in order not to be afraid and, of course, his or her deep hurt is protected by fear. If these reactions happened very early, they become hidden memories. Even if they don't but are repeated often enough, we don't become aware we are enacting them. Just like breathing – we are not conscious most of the time of the fact that we breathe – these reactions become automatic.

The survival reaction to pain is based on fear; this is like a wordless memory, a *feeling fear memory* that is established in the brain in the form of biological connections. It isn't understood intellectually and can't be remembered as a real memory. This *feeling fear memory* can be triggered easily by stimuli in the environment; for example, a simple telephone call, which turns out to be a wrong number or someone who has no time to talk to us, could trigger depression because the unending feelings are of fear of rejection – 'no one is interested in me'. This *fear feeling* is a warning signal that the system is in danger of pain. Triggers, such as unreturned phone calls ('he or she doesn't want to talk to me'), are not real now but were real during the time the child felt the pain of rejection and, consequently, fear of such pain.

We can see the painful experiences to which we have been exposed (such as abandonment, punishment, neglect, abuse, feeling unloved and uncared for) as the result of being brought up by depressed parents. Because the child isn't able to make sense of their painful experiences, they become immediately afraid in order to survive. These fear reactions are hidden memories, too.

Sometimes when we become anxious about life and frightened for no reason at all, it is the fear that is protecting us. The fear is connected to our hidden memory of pain and is a means of safeguarding us. Fear is a greater challenge because it is what most of us habitually try to run away from or avoid feeling. Consequently, we develop another brain reaction to try to halt our fears. This reaction may result in us adopting diverse techniques to avoid being hurt. These reactions could be to resist, compromise, use aggression and even attack people, conform, hold back, speak too much or not speak at all. We adopt such strategies as attempts to overcome our fears. Unfortunately, such strategies serve only to increase our fears and we end up achieving the opposite. Life becomes a constant battle of running away from fear, which is a bigger fear, of course, and we create more fears in the process. The more we run, the stronger the fear; if we fight the fear, it gets even stronger.

*When you fight war with war you never win.*

## Our *Protector*

We have now established that painful feelings are memories created in the system before we had the ability to make sense of them. As a result of the painful experience, neural pathways are activated simultaneously and become associated with each other to form patterns of fear reactions. These patterns of reactions are mental processes created by neural firing: the creation of neural connections that are retained in hidden (implicit) memory, in which experiences and adaptations are created in response to danger. Over the years the brain becomes a master at adapting to the demands of our surroundings by developing what I have dubbed our *Protector*. The brain responds to these fear experiences with further organization of neuron connections in order to protect us from the pain that we don't understand, and in an attempt to avoid the fears, too.

Behaviours such as being withdrawn, quiet, timid, depressed, angry and acting dangerously or aggressively are our *Protector's* responses to the pain and fear of being unloved. This can also happen in our adult lives at any time when we feel we might be rejected. The brain can also be paralyzed, not wanting to feel the pain and hurt again. We can become afraid of what people will do to us. In relationships, the deep, buried feelings of previous rejections can mean that we unconsciously live in fear that our partner will leave us and we will be alone. We may therefore use protective behaviours that can be full of contradictions. For example, we say 'yes' and smile but we actually mean 'no'; we may smile when listening to criticism or upon hearing bad news; we might also agree to do things for people while inside we actually don't want to do them at all; we can get angry, aggressive and tell lies.

These failed attempts are, in fact, survival mechanisms designed to protect us from fear, while the fear itself is designed to protect us as children from pain. As we grow older, these survival mechanisms remain and become protective behaviours – literally, behaviours we use for our protection. Fear becomes like a signal telling us that the deep primal pains are very close. Fear then suppresses the pain. In other words, it tells the pain to go away, 'to keep me safe' and our *Protector* does the same by suppressing the fear. In other words, it is also telling the fear to go away; 'I don't want to be afraid'. So, what works for us as children can work against us as adults.

All these reactions are a mask that suppresses and seeks to avoid expression of our fears. Such adaptations and coping defence mechanisms manifest themselves in different ways to reflect various situations. At the same time these hidden memories are organized in a different way to real or imagined danger reactions. The pain of our childhood memories can be seen in every expression on our faces and in every cell of our bodies. In our attempts not to feel the pain and fear we put on a mask to conceal it. The pain, however, then becomes even stronger *because* we are trying to suppress it. The human brain functions to support our survival. It may not be effective, however, as such survival reactions can also limit us.

Our early experience in the womb is the first stage of creating our survival protection. If the mother is going through any difficult experiences and feels bad throughout her pregnancy, then the unborn child can perceive its environment as unwelcoming. This experience represents the first time that the child feels rejection. The unborn baby can tune into the thoughts and dreams of the mother and this adds another fundamental variable to the creation of the *Protector*. When the child is born, they are predisposed by their unconscious memory that interacts with new painful experiences after the birth. Such a predisposition enforces the protective character. This predisposition, however, can be healed if the child isn't subjected to painful experiences after birth.

We have looked at the brain's role of protecting us from hurtful experiences as a strategy that protects our survival in our early lives. We therefore learn to present ourselves to the world through a mask in order to survive, which is the ultimate goal for humans. So, in order to start healing and to take steps to find *the real you,* we need to explore and understand better how our hidden memories affect us and operate within us. In the next chapter we will look at understanding the results of these hidden memories and start to manage them rather than suppressing or fighting them. In other words, we will feel them, understand their origins and release them so we are no longer limited by them and we can become who we really are.

# CHAPTER 4
# OUR MECHANICAL RESPONSE MECHANISM (THE *PROTECTOR*)

*Our* Protector *defends us by constantly changing the masks we wear in order to adapt to every threatening situation.*

## The *Protector*

Our *Protector* utilizes many avoidance strategies in order to keep us from feeling pain and to help us survive. In real-life situations and at any time that we lose concentration or lose being in the moment, our *Protector* can take over or hijack us. At these times our *Protector* is in full control of our actions. Our actions become a reaction to past consciously *un*remembered situations. Over time, the *Protector* develops by constantly training to become another character in its own right, a mask we wear to protect ourselves and at the same time hide who we really are. After wearing the mask for a long time, we no longer know the difference between who we really are and the mask or the difference between who we are and whom we think we are. This way of managing our feelings can be compared to playing a game or acting in a drama that we cannot ever control. Imagine an actor who plays the same role for 30 or 40 years; we become like that actor who has mastered his or her act by constantly repeating the lines, the movements, the patterns of interactions and the reactions to those around us. Such repetition makes us perfect actors in the play of life and perfect players in the game of life.

The director is our unconscious self that directs us to play a role from which we may not be able to escape. Not only that, but we will look for people who represent those people from our past who hurt us, for example, and cast them in our play in the parts others have played in the past. We act out a drama with them on the stage of day-to-day interactions. We are more than likely to imagine them as the people who hurt us, or make them conform to the roles we expect of them. Some people may even yield to our expectations if our game is powerful enough.

Over the years, our *Protector* masters a pattern of survival that allows us to suppress our fears. We become skillful actors in the play of life and our masks conceal our fears. The constant repetition creates a new personality that conforms to the mask or to a personality. We can no longer separate ourselves from our mask; in fact, the word *person* comes from the Latin word 'persona', meaning mask – a mask that we sometimes have to wear in society. Of course, sometimes we have to be political and we have to use this persona. For example, in the workplace we may compromise with our boss because we feel unsafe but confront the people who work under us because we feel safer.

The problem with wearing a mask is that it filters our perception of reality by our unconscious, compulsive activity of escaping the pain of dealing with others. It takes a great deal of energy to keep the fear repressed and to stop painful buried feelings from overwhelming us. After wearing the mask for a long time, we fail to realize that we are wearing a mask and cannot separate ourselves from it.

*'Each of us harbours in our inner universe a number of "characters", parts of ourselves that frequently operate in complete contradiction to one another, causing conflict and mental pain to our conscious selves.'*
JOYCE MCDOUGALL, *THEATERS OF THE MIND,*
*ILLUSION AND TRUTH ON THE PSYCHOANALYTIC STAGE*

## The role of our *Protector*

Protective behaviour has many layers and can manifest itself in many different roles, depending on the context in which we find ourselves. In relationships, for example, protection can manifest as compromising too much or doing too much for our partner, more than we do for ourselves. This is a protective reaction to past subconscious reactions to pain and fear of rejection. The same protection can also manifest as being very kind, too accepting and not voicing our opinion about what we want in the relationship. These protections can even go as far as extreme neurotic symptoms of worrying about partners or children, or being overprotective and panicking about a partner when they are ill. All of these protective behaviours can be reactions to pain and fear of loss. Protection can also manifest itself as aggression, anger and impulsive decision-making, which are all reactions to past unconscious neglect or sense of abandonment.

We can also see protective behaviours in people who fight for some cause, whether it be for freedom, peace or the underprivileged, in an obsessive way. Of course, it is absolutely right to support worthy causes but what I am talking about is a kind of obsession about *saving* other people or causes in a neurotic way or trying to make peace at any cost.

Again, this kind of protection is a reaction to past experiences of injustice. The protection can also appear in the form of being a perfectionist and trying to be in control. Again, this can be a reaction to immaturity when children at a young age had to grow up too quickly and were not stimulated in a loving way. For example, when they could not do something or made mistakes and no one told them that it is OK to fail, as this is the way we learn. These children were left to try to fix many things on their own. They may have had unavailable parents or parents who were brought up in exactly the same way; it is likely that the parents themselves were not stimulated as children either and therefore could not give their children what they were not capable of doing themselves. They teach their children to adopt the same protection, too.

This kind of protection can also manifest itself in being very independent and being unable to receive support, as well as an inability to relate to partners in relationships and difficulties in work partnerships. These children grow up having developed a *Protector* that means they work alone most of the time and find it hard to function in partnership or in teams. They grow up giving up too soon or building up a protection of recovering too fast when facing similar situations of loss. Their *Protector* is trying to be strong as a reaction to suppress their painful memories of being unable to cope alone. Ironically, they tend to end up being alone anyway. An extreme example of this type of protection would be a 'holy' mask, which a person wears by taking a vow to be celibate, live alone and become very spiritual. He or she could be suppressing their pain and fear of rejection but this becomes an extraordinary escape because he or she cannot actually tolerate living an ordinary life where they risk loving someone and being rejected.

> *'We do not readily escape the roles that are essentially ours. Each of us is drawn into an unfolding life drama in which the plot reveals itself in an uncannily repetitive way.'*
> JOYCE MCDOUGALL, *THEATERS OF THE MIND, ILLUSION AND TRUTH ON THE PSYCHOANALYTIC STAGE*

This shows that we unconsciously write our own scripts, anticipate the plots and attract people to where they are performed. All of this was prepared a long time ago when we were children through the ways we experienced the world and the resultant assumptions regarding our future. Our main motivation when we are children is to survive as best we can and we do not understand that we are creating a plot and a script for the future. We can then spend the rest of our lives looking for the cast in order to fulfil our dreams on the stage of life and they often appear in our relationships. Later on, in times of stress, all the unresolved painful experiences provide us with the drama that unfolds as the unconscious compulsive acting out of a protective character.

Ironically, such an unconscious compulsion is activated to escape suffering and to avoid fear, spanning years of repetition, which has allowed pain to exist by suppressing it. Our *Protector* is the key to understanding how we have become whom we think we are and how we can transform our limitations to become what we really are.

Before any attempts can be made to deal with our *Protector*, we need to explore the dynamics of our *Protector* in our brain and how such processes limit us. The job of the *Protector* is to suppress and resist fear and pain. Unfortunately, such resistance is more painful than the fear and pain themselves and often fools us into believing that the pain isn't there any more. At the same time the pain hurts more when we try to block it and we risk becoming numb. We suffer the consequences of living life by acting out our protective behaviours. The price we pay can be that we don't achieve what we want in life.

Our *Protector* will constantly challenge us about what we are afraid of and how we focus on getting rid of fear. Ironically, this focus will attract situations that match our fears. Even if we don't attract such stimuli, we will generate a false perception that misrepresents the stimuli and will change them into an object of fear. We may then become attached to our fears and our perception of them.

## There is nothing to fear but fear itself

If you have a fear of loneliness, you will see loneliness everywhere you go and may even become lonely and suffer until you give it up. If you are afraid of being poor, you will see poverty. Life will invite poverty or people into your life who are poor, because your fear will attract into your life the experience of being in a relationship with poor people.

Alternatively, you may have a relationship with people who will cause you to lose what money you have. This pattern will keep on recurring until you no longer have the fear.

The human brain is constantly interacting with others, and so we should begin our understanding of our *Protector* and what controls it by observing our reactions and the meanings that arise from these interactions.

The relationship between memory and our *Protector* is crucial here. Our hidden memory appears as experiences of our present reality. Such memories create a world of reactions organized by our past-internalized experiences. When this memory is triggered by stimuli, protective behaviours manifest themselves, as we are flooded with deep emotional reactions that rapidly shift our state of mind. We can freeze, go into a trance, explode with rage, or cry. We can be out of control and react in a way in which we would not ordinarily choose to behave. Such hidden protective behaviours, reactions and defence mechanisms distort reality in order to achieve the goal of reducing fear. These protective behaviours are also unconscious memories used in the past to control our anxiety and fear so that we can feel safe.

> '*Every time we choose safety, we reinforce fear.*'
> CHERI HUBER, ZEN TEACHER AND WRITER

Our *Protector* is activated by stimuli in the environment or in relationships, in the presence of certain people or situations, or in an experience that is similar to a past experience. It suppresses the experience of pain, fear and emotion. The deep unconscious memory of pain and fear embedded in our lives influences our perceptions, emotions, behaviours and physical sensations throughout time – present, past and future. These are old neural networks of memories that don't have a sense of time or age and linger in their original form. They also have no sense of self. When they are recalled, we don't feel a sense of something being recalled, as the *Protector* flows in immediately to suppress the pain. And again, after many years of repeating the protective behaviours, the brain has formed a neural network of defences. The *Protector* is also made up of connections in the brain.

## The rationale behind our protective behaviours

Professor Hugo Critchley, co-director of the Sackler Centre for Consciousness Science at Brighton and Sussex Medical School, suggests that in the absence of adequate assistance from others in making sense of our emotions when we were young, the brain organizes itself into a variety of coping strategies and defence mechanisms.

Let me give a brief description of what I am talking about here. In a family where a family member (one of the parents, for example) disappears or leaves without much explanation, or a child is rejected by one or both parents, the child may not make sense of their loss; the child simply does not understand, but feels the loss. They tend to grow up developing a strategy of giving up too soon in relationships, particularly if they feel any sign of rejection, or can build up a protection of moving on too fast or speedily recovering when facing similar situations of loss, without allowing themselves to feel any pain. In these situations, the *Protector* is trying to prevent them from feeling the pain again as a reaction to suppress painful memories of loss. These children grow up looking for love like anyone else but when they get close to someone in a relationship, their body remembers the pain of loss and rejection, their *Protector* kicks in and they run away from the relationship at the same time that they really need it. The *Protector* will not allow them to love or commit to a partner, in order to protect them from another painful experience of rejection. It is really important here to emphasize that the strategy they adopt, guided by the *Protector*, is not in the conscious mind but in the subconscious mind. These children can consequently remain alone as adults: the very thing they are trying to avoid. This is a clear example of how our intentions contradict our actions.

If at the time, however, the child receives adequate assistance and support to understand what happened to the family member by someone explaining the reasons for the absence of this person and allowing them to express their feelings and anxiety, then they begin to make sense of their emotions. They can feel their emotion and feel safe that the feelings are OK and they can develop the ability to move the experience to the past. Otherwise, the pain remains untouched and there remains a fear of facing the pain. The *Protector* develops defences to try to achieve the goal of reducing anxiety and fear.

Another example: if a parent suddenly disappears without saying goodbye or dies suddenly, the child loses the connection very fast without making any sense of it. The intense separation anxiety and fear is in the child's mind forever and so they develop a protective mechanism to avoid feeling such pain again by being very independent or ending relationships quickly when conflict arises and moving fast to try and create other, new connections.

Another form of protection is to get as many people to stay with them as they can by being very giving. They give so that people will stay with them, or they may even have many partners because they do not trust anyone to stay or do not believe that anyone might love them enough to stay with them. You can see how painful these feelings are and how we do not want to feel them again, but they never fade away with time; in fact, they get stronger.

A client who came to me had an unusual relationship pattern. She wanted a loving relationship very badly but whenever someone became close to her, she felt numb and unapproachable, and men did not want to be with her. This client had a very good relationship with her parents and did not suffer any separation during childhood. This left me extremely puzzled as to how this form of protection could have formed in her brain. During our work together she mentioned that when she was born she developed an illness and was taken away from her mother and put in an incubator for a few weeks. During this time her mother was not able to see her very much or touch her. As a baby she developed severe separation anxiety and fear without the ability to make any sense of it. The consequences were that whenever a loving man appeared in her life, her brain reacted to protect her from separation and she numbed the pain by becoming numb and therefore unavailable.

According to research in child development, a common pattern observed among children who were abandoned by a parent is that they did not understand what happened at the time and when reunited with the parent, they would reject him or her to avoid being rejected again. Rejecting the person they love very much creates a rejecting protective character. In this instance, the *Protector's* strategy is to reject the one we love the most. Such children may grow up wanting love and a happy relationship, but as soon as they experience love for a partner, it triggers the pain and fear of abandonment. The protection could show itself through anger, being judgemental, rejection or even aggression. Obviously the partner does not understand this and often reacts in a way that reinforces the protection. This is another example that clearly shows why and how our intentions can contradict our behaviour.

You can see from the examples above how the *Protector* is our defence made up by neurological connections in the brain, which shapes every aspect of our lives and our relationships. The irony here is that while our painful experiences of the past have ended, our responses and reactions still remain in our unconscious hidden memory and manifest repeatedly in our conscious daily lives and relationships under the guise of the *Protector*. We live with a constant strategy of damage control. The key message here is that not making sense of an experience means it is unresolved and incomplete. Consequently, our reactions keep repeating like a tape recorder in our subconscious.

Heather Berlin and Christof Koch's psychodynamic theory suggests that there is an unconscious dynamic that processes defensively, removing anxiety-provoking thoughts and impulses from our consciousness. These processes, which keep unwanted thoughts from entering our consciousness, are known as defence mechanisms and include repression, suppression and dissociation. This is our protective behaviour's main purpose: to suppress any pain that is anxiety-provoking. This idea of suppression goes back even to Sigmund Freud, the father of psychoanalysis, as the means of pushing unwanted, anxiety-provoking thoughts, memories, emotions, fantasies and desires out of conscious awareness.

> *If a child doesn't understand how to cope with pain, there is fear. If they can't understand how to deal with fear, it is because they weren't given any assistance in doing so by parents and family. In order to cope with this painful experience, they develop another layer of protection, which is the* Protector.

These patterns of protection spread into every area of our lives – for example, our interactions in relationships, business, career, parenting, decision-making, etc. They organize what we embrace and what we avoid in life. These patterns also become the basis on which we focus our attention, as well as the assumptions that we make about situations, future experiences and people. We might use these coping defence strategies throughout our lifetime and they play a major role in how we make decisions and how we limit ourselves or miss out on opportunities in life.

If we look carefully at all our experiences and patterns in relationships, we can see how our protective behaviours reproduce events over and over again. We will find a theme that runs through everything we do in life. For example, when we grow up watching a family interacting in a certain way and we react to situations in certain ways, we develop a pattern of coping that is similar to the pattern of coping used by the people who took care of us. Then, later, we leave home and meet someone with different ways of coping. This may result in conflict because our *Protector* is functioning based on the rehearsal it received and learned to cope with family conflicts in the way ours did.

Conflict arises because our brain has been shaped in every possible way to react to, expect and anticipate what should happen in a relationship. We then immediately target the other person in the relationship. In fact, we can go as far as blaming the other person for the very thing from which we are actually suffering unconsciously. Our brain will only see people in the way it has been trained to see them. The relationship becomes a battlefield, as each person tries to win the other over to his or her way of thinking. What is even more crucial is that the brain is trained to look outside itself, but not at itself and, therefore, we will find fault in others until we can look inside ourselves.

## The hidden dynamic of the *Protector*

All these defence strategies make us feel, perceive and act in certain ways to protect ourselves from fear. We end up compromising and limiting ourselves in every action we undertake in life. These constructs of the defence mechanism are like armour we wear. They are adaptations against real or imagined danger in order to stop us feeling fear. We live life playing the game of trying not to be found out. Human beings employ many ways of escape, either by suppressing fear, running away from it or by freezing. Freud stated that these defences are ways in which the brain networks have organized themselves to face difficulties. These defences are thoughts, feelings and behaviours that are prevented from being integrated within our conscious awareness.

Our *Protector* often takes the form of unconscious compulsive actions in order to escape pain by suppressing our fear. When we perceive rejection from another person, it can induce a shift in our mental state. The rejection reminds us of our childhood. The feeling of rejection and the association with our hidden memories from past experiences induces a behavioural impulse to flee as, for example, from an angry parent or a depressed mother. It also can induce physical sensations of tension and pain. These links are made very quickly without our conscious awareness and without the feeling that we are recalling anything.

> *'A great many human activities are performed (for both good and ill) in order to win acceptance from others.'*
> RANDALL PARKER, *BRAIN SCANS SHOW REJECTION CAUSES PAIN SIMILAR TO PHYSICAL PAIN* (14 OCTOBER 2003), *BIOLOGICAL MIND*

To gain the approval of others, our *Protector* may masquerade as a lovable person in order to hide the fear of rejection or of being alone, as well as the fear of the primal pain of abandonment. Hiding behind a mask of pride that declares 'I want to be alone' or 'I don't need anyone' is also a means of taking shelter from the fear that the pain of rejection causes.

We can also wear the mask of the *Rescuer*, helping people in order to cover our fear of abandonment and need to be saved. We attempt to achieve a feeling of being needed by others. Our *Protector* manifests itself as controlling people by loving and helping them or rescuing people too much. Displaying this behaviour can indicate that a person is trying to give people what they themselves lacked in their childhood but do not want to risk asking for themselves in case they are rejected. In this way, they feel in control, although actually the *Protector* is in charge and the chances of rejection are 0 per cent.

Our *Protector* often interacts with other people's *Protectors* and they can reinforce one another. For example, if we have a fear of loss, we may have developed a *Protector* with the reaction of holding on to things and not letting go; due to this fear, we may also avoid spending money. We might then attract someone who has the same fear of loss but hides their fear of receiving by pretending to be generous and spending our money.

The protective personality will attract people to us who possess a similar dynamic. Each will activate the other's *Protector*. We can also change people by means of our *Protector*, and vice versa. Our *Protector* has an impact on people and, if we are powerful enough, we can influence them and even change the way they treat us. If we succeed in getting them to play our game, however, we lose. In other words, we hurt ourselves more by allowing people to treat us as less than we are. We can judge others' behaviour based on their personality, but when it comes to ourselves, we explain our behaviour based on the environment that has caused it rather than as a game we are playing. It is as if we have a blind spot when it comes to looking at ourselves.

> 'It is I alone who frame on those lips the words that may hurt me.'
> NILAKANTA SRI RAM (1889–1973),
> INDIAN TEACHER, WRITER AND THEOSOPHIST

Some people continue to be afraid, neurotic and anxious because they are afraid to get in touch with their fears. It is fear of getting in touch with the pain of their earliest unmet needs for love and care. Such defences can be projected into phobias, such as cleaning too much or fear of (the complete opposite of a phobia) self-neglect. We can wear a multitude of masks. Some of the neurotic behaviours are the result of a child's past response to danger; these past responses are still alive in the present.

Another extreme case of the reaction to fear can be fighting for a cause or fighting injustice. Most people who fight for justice and fight for peace, for instance, are actually angry and afraid of past experiences when an aggressive and armed person harmed them or a family member. Their *Protector* may be masquerading as a defender of the weak fighting an oppressor. It is very likely that some of these people are angry at not being loved in the first place and so they project their pain on to a fight for other people whom they perceive as similarly unloved or badly treated. Justice cannot develop while judging others. The reason we have wars is that we judge the people against whom we are fighting. Judging can be an aspect of the *Protector*, too.

We can be fanatical in trying to convince others of something of which we aren't sure ourselves. When we have faith in what we are doing, we don't have to convince anyone about anything. Wishing to change others – or the world is in itself an act of oppression and suppression of our trapped feelings. When we truly feel free, we never even have to talk about freedom. Only people who are in prison want to escape.

If children have been humiliated or are not loved or respected, they may attempt to run away from painful experiences in their past by adopting dangerous and destructive reactions toward people. They may grow up to adopt extreme political beliefs, which support violent means to achieve their ends. Many extremists, racists and fanatical groups are based on self-harm and do not support anyone. These people are often looking for an enemy to fight and to avenge themselves for the pain they themselves suffered.

If we truly want peace, we need to identify with what is peaceful within us. This act will bring peace to the world. Living a life of inner peace will eventually overcome all outer conflicts and war. We cannot stop any war unless we are first free of the war inside ourselves.

Our *Protector* is a dynamic trying to suppress our internal war. This makes us perceive everything outside as a war. There is a need for us to change our perception of the world, which is based on a hidden memory of injustice, hurts and disappointments. If we manage this change, then tolerance will emerge and allow us to bear injustice and face it without fighting it. Tolerance does not come through learning, but through insight.

*'The only devils are those in our hearts.'*
MAHATMA GANDHI

## The hidden war

*The* Protector *allows our unconscious reactions to our past hidden memories to create a future of hidden unconscious, false expectations that fight reality.*

Each one of us is the entire world; there is a message for us here on how to overcome the war inside ourselves just by looking at the world around us in a different way. All attempts to bring about peace in the world have failed simply because our inner *Protectors* are fighting for peace.

We don't like war and we judge the nations, people, races and countries that are fighting. The word 'peace' means a hidden war because as long as we are fighting to achieve it, it is actually another war. The world does not need desperate attempts at peacemaking; it does not need to fight for peace. Instead, we need an evolution of human consciousness to enable us to rise above the idea of trying to find peace at all, even so far as accepting war as part of that evolution. This is an important point to remember when we look at healing our *Protector*. Our *Protector* can also pretend to be peaceful, but unless we recognize the awesome pressure of the fear, pain and war within us that compels us to fight, we can never understand what causes our war. The mask of the peacemaker hides the intolerant pain of conflict.

> *'We must not fight injustice, we must make it visible.'*
> MAHATMA GANDHI

Another aspect of our *Protector's* expression is demonstrated in our attempts to help or save people and try to take their pain away. Conversely, the opposite is the projecting of our fears on to others and judging them for the same things we don't like about ourselves.

It is very important to emphasize that our *Protector* is brought about by neurological connections induced by our reactions to fear, manifesting themselves as a form of defence. They are only reactions, not who we are. These reactions have the power to shape our lives by selecting what we approach and what we avoid, as we live by running away from pain and searching for love and comfort. These patterns of relating to others are coping strategies and our defences may be in place for a lifetime. They seem to have a mind of their own and it can also seem that we have no ability to control them.

Almost all of our interactions with others are filtered through the lens of past, which has created mental models of painful experiences in the past. We are constantly inviting the past unconscious memory into the present; therefore we are more likely to experience past painful feelings in the present without being conscious that these have already happened in the past. For instance, when we compromise in relationships and agree to things that we don't want, these are false attempts to protect our body, mind and emotions from danger. These reactions move by themselves and live in opposition to our conscious intentions. Sometimes we identify with them and begin to believe this is who we are and then judge ourselves. Recall the many times you have said to yourself 'I am not strong', 'I am not capable' or 'this must be who I am'. Believing such statements is the beginning of creating a false story about you.

After years of repetition our *Protector* causes us to develop ideas about who we are and we live with those ideas rather than appreciating our immediate and present experience of living in the *now*. We fail to realize that who we really are is far more than this.

The *Protector* can influence the way we anticipate the way people will behave toward us, so that we develop perceptions to react even before they hurt us. These perceptions become powerful images and we live with these images in our relationships rather than living in the immediate experience – the *now* – that actually exists between human beings. Our *Protector* has developed in such a way as to define our life and who we are, and we therefore also define other people and who *they* are by the ways we allow them to treat us.

We live with a strategy of damage control even though there is no longer any damage. It is as if we continue to fight a war that has already ended.

There was a fascinating story on the news from the 1950s, which serves to illustrate how our old reactions continue to affect us in our present daily lives. It was about some Japanese soldiers attacking tourists in the South Pacific long after World War II had ended. The Japanese Navy had apparently left soldiers behind on many small islands throughout the Pacific and forgotten about them. Some five years later, pleasure craft would innocently land on these islands only to be attacked by soldiers who still believed the war was going on. The soldiers had dutifully kept their guns oiled and remained vigilant for decades in anticipation of attack. They were fighting a war that actually no longer existed. As late as 1951, the Japanese soldiers were holding out on these islands. They refused to believe the war was over and resisted every attempt by the Navy to remove them.

Like these Japanese soldiers, our early hidden memories keep the struggle alive, holding on to stress and trauma from a time before we can remember, because the brain is not able to understand what the *war* was about. Our conscious awareness may move on to new life challenges, but our hidden memory retains our initial reactions to fear and pain. You can see how the brain functions here: it uses a pattern of activity previously associated with fear, which in the present can react to false signals. Our *Protector* is still vigilant for any sign of attack. We misunderstand people's intentions and reactions toward us and we react as if we are still at war when we explode in retaliation. Our hidden memories in the subconscious are refusing to believe that the war is over and we keep on going and fighting it.

If we could (metaphorically speaking) find a way to land on the beaches of our deep unconscious, convince the loyal soldiers trapped deep in the subconscious mind (our hidden memories) that the war is over and allow ourselves to feel the pain and still feel safe at the same time, then the war would truly end. Probably the most famous of the Japanese holdouts, Onoda, was the only survivor of a group of four. He surrendered 29 years after Japan's formal surrender and 15 years after he was declared legally dead in Japan. When he accepted that the war was over, he openly wept. In his weeping was the beginning of feeling the pain of the war and the realization that it was all over; he was then able to experience the healing and acceptance of his past trauma. I will explore this phenomenon later, in Part II.

Our early memories react like the Japanese soldiers, retaining trauma from the past. Each time we react in the same way, the memory is modified and gets stronger. While we consciously try to move on, our hidden memory retains outdated protective behaviour, ever vigilant for signs of attack. When we are under threat, we can literally attack people to protect ourselves, sometimes also retreating to protect ourselves. Unconscious memory always takes us to the past and conscious memory always takes us to the now.

Now we can see why we react so quickly and strongly to certain situations: we have a very strong unconscious memory and a small conscious memory. Memory is easily retrieved when the emotional state we were in when the memory was formed matches our current emotional state. We are more likely to remember sad events when we are depressed, for example. The more similar the pattern of activation is during the experience, the more the unconscious memory is likely to surface.

> *'Wild animals run from the dangers they actually see,*
> *and once they have escaped them they worry no more.*
> *We, however, are tormented by what we saw in the*
> *past and what is to come.'*
> SENECA

People who suffer from depression often see everything in a negative way. Hidden memory affects their perceptions and expectations of what they see in the present and how they see the future.

An interesting experiment was conducted on depression, involving a group of depressed subjects and a control group of non-depressed subjects. Both groups were given words to memorize. Both groups were then given a memory test and it was found that the depressed group recalled more negative words than the control group. We can see here that the hidden memory was already primed to connect with negative feelings, which helped the depressed subjects to recall the negative words more easily.

During our interpersonal interactions, we automatically have reflex reactions to reduce our anxiety by saying something positive so that we don't get hurt. Some people even say negative things in order to avoid being hurt. Our *Protector* reveals itself through all kinds of coping defences to help us avoid facing our deepest pain. This makes our life feel like we are running away from something that no longer exists. This constant running can also cause us suffering but these reactions are very difficult to change because they are shaped during our earliest development as an adaptation against a real or imagined danger. It is an early defence at all levels of the nervous system and has become encoded in our entire being in sensory, motor and emotional networks as protection against any real or imagined danger in the present.

> *'Our interactions with one another reflect a dance between love and fear.'*
> RAM DASS, AMERICAN SPIRITUAL TEACHER AND AUTHOR

## Love and fear

Have we become victims of our past? The bottom line here is our desire for love and our avoidance of pain at all costs.

Our desperate attempts to be loved and to avoid pain can masquerade in behaviour that is seeking to be loved because we are afraid of being disliked for who we think we are. Someone who thinks he or she is unlovable will try to get as much love as possible. This is based on a primal experience of pain of rejection and separation. Ironically, if we are willing to be disliked for who we really are, others will like us. Many of us end up doing many things and behaving in certain ways in order to hide our fear of not getting the love we need. Some of these behaviours, however, can make people actually stop loving us because we are not being authentic and so we get what we don't want. No one can love you if you become someone else (wear a mask) in order to be loved by him or her.

Family dynamics can create feelings of separation and rejection. For example, a parent who is very busy and unavailable most of the time may unwittingly communicate to the child that his or her personal life is more important than being with their child or even caring for them. If a child isn't able to make sense of the absence and therefore the loss of the parent, they may feel the pain of loneliness. In extreme cases, a child may begin to protect itself by isolating itself more. They may talk to themselves and make up stories because there is no one there to soothe and calm them, encourage, support and protect them. From the child's perspective, the parent has made other things in his or her life more important. As an adult, this child may live an isolated life as a protection against feeling the pain of feeling neglected and this causes the child even more pain.

If the child doesn't have the parent around or another loving carer, they may grow up with no foundation of love and develop a powerful *Protector* that makes it difficult for them to commit to anyone later in life. The stress for the child is that they have developed a pattern of constantly seeking love and attention but their needs are only fulfilled by material possessions, such as toys. In later life, this may develop into all-consuming needs for, perhaps, a new car, new clothes, sex or drugs, while the need for love dominates every aspect of his or her life and there is no escape.

## The *Protector's* defensive behaviour patterns

Some children go on trying to work harder to please their parents or rebel and get depressed as a reaction from avoiding the painful memories of abandonment. The child might adopt a similar defence pattern to his or her parents by trying to do the same things they did. In other words, the child will develop the same *Protector* as his or her parents. Even more ironically and paradoxically, when this child grows up and has a family, they may not have enough time for their children because they can't give what they haven't experienced. But the failure of this child as a parent can set them up on a journey of self-healing if they pay attention to how their *Protector* operates and the consequences of the *Protector's* defensive behaviour patterns.

A child who watches his or her parents fighting is not afraid of the fighting; they are afraid of the family falling apart and that no one will be home to look after them. They may feel insecure and develop a *Protector* who avoids conflict at all costs. Or they may don the mask of the peacemaker. They may even end up as a peace campaigner or a mediator between people. His or her actual intentions may not be about people at all; they will be about not wanting to experience the pain of separation.

In another situation, if a child witnesses one of the parents threatening to leave the family home, the child may grow up to be afraid of life and death because they have taken on board the association that people may leave. Their model of relationships is therefore painful and they may employ sabotaging techniques to ensure that they leave relationships before the other person can leave.

Most people develop many ways of coping with a range of frightening situations. Some might try to be submissive toward angry people, while others become overwhelmed in circumstances that others would consider to be only minimally stressful. Fear of ridicule might cause them to shake uncontrollably when called upon to speak in public, or a terror of strangers might lead them to hide at home, unable to work or go out shopping. Many people can fall prey to fear, which of course can be temporarily overcome by the inner *Protector*.

Initially we develop our *Protector* in order to protect ourselves, but as we grow older it takes over and begins to dominate our interactions with people. Over the years, we have created our identity, heavily predisposed by our *Protector* and influenced by our reactions to life events and our cultural environment.

# CHAPTER 5
# THE STORY, SCRIPT AND ACT WE USE TO HIDE OUR TRUE SELVES

*We first create our* Protector *and then*
*our* Protector *creates us.*

## Playing a role

Over the years, we create some form of self-identity, heavily predisposed by our *Protector* and influenced by our reactions to most life events and culture. We have become like actors playing on the stage of life. Most of the time we are not aware that we are on a stage hiding our true self. After years of playing the role, we become the actors, directors, scriptwriters and authors of our lives. We begin to create the story of who we think we are, learn the script by heart and forget who we really are.

Stories are, in fact, self-deceptions because they serve to keep our awareness away from those feelings that are most relevant, but less acceptable. Everyone is organized around a story, which, as it repeats itself throughout our life, becomes a play. After years of telling and acting the story of our unhappy childhood experiences and events, we unconsciously become masterful actors in a show that goes on each day. And the lead character is the *Protector*. These repetitions simply serve to strengthen old brain connections. The more we repeat these patterns, the stronger the connections become. We need to ask ourselves: when will the time come to end the old story and begin a real one?

> '*Our inner characters are constantly seeking a stage on which to play out their tragedies and comedies. Although we rarely assume responsibility for our secret theatre productions, the producer is seated in our own mind.*'
> JOYCE MCDOUGALL, *THEATERS OF THE MIND,*
> *ILLUSION AND TRUTH ON THE PSYCHOANALYTIC STAGE*

In order for us to find consistent love in a world full of disappointments and inconsistencies, we desperately place ourselves within the context of a story in an attempt to define ourselves. This is especially true of people living in Western societies, where we are at risk of losing a sense of belonging to group connections and cultures. We frantically try to place ourselves within a story in order to find consistency in an infinite number of contexts and to create a way of being in the world. Our *Protector* has become real in our story from the way it reacts to others in relationships and responds to how others react to us. It has played a part in creating a false sense of identity in our minds, based on the reactions of others and our reactions to them.

The perceptions of others are almost always communicated to us by the way they treat us, what they say to us and think of us. People can change us too, as we can actually unconsciously conform to what they expect us to be, even though that *persona* is a negative one. This is another, deeper level of the *Protector* and we believe this about ourselves, too. Each thought or observation is then confirmed around the idea that we have formed of ourselves.

This image we accumulate of ourselves becomes internalized and we begin to act according to the image we have created, especially in our relationships with others. We can find that we have different self-images in different contexts – our *Protector* plays many roles – and, for instance, in our place of work we may behave differently to when we are with our partners. Our reactions may shift in the presence of our parents, no matter how old we are and no matter how determined we are not to. This is because we are triggered by the intensity of the hidden memory that occurred in our relationship with them in the past. These personas become a problem when we feel that we no longer are ourselves and our actions are actually having a negative effect on our relationships, work or ability to achieve our true potential.

## Constructing a story

Again, this is very important in understanding how our *Protector* can limit us even before anything happens to us. Therefore, what we are actually experiencing is the story we have constructed around a difficult situation and the fear this might evoke in us. Our story becomes a psychological lens, which distorts our perception of reality. A vicious cycle begins as our fears are linked to the story we have made up. Understanding the idea of having a script or story is extremely important here, as it creates false realities.

This following example shows how far our story can go, the consequences of living in a story and how we can lose ourselves in the stories we tell ourselves.

I worked with a client who had severe traumas in her childhood. She was punished a lot and unfortunately experienced similar situations in her career, marriage and choice of friends. Unsurprisingly, over the years she had created a story that the world was unsafe to live in. This story originated in her family life and her childhood. The story she developed over the years was that everybody wanted to punish her, including the organizations and social services monitoring her. She was so clear about her story, which she had constructed since childhood, that she built it up to a clear conviction.

In various sessions with her, her entire focus was on her relationships and the men who lied and wanted to punish her. She even suspected her neighbours and believed her extended family was only after her money. Even when her son grew up, she began to believe that he wanted to punish her, too. She did not trust any professionals to support her and she was trapped in a cycle of perpetually running from a fear that she had created. William James expressed this dynamic very well when he said, *'We don't run from the bear because we are afraid. Instead we feel afraid because we run.'*

Of course, we all do the same, to a lesser or greater degree. It is helpful to pay attention to our thoughts, what occupies our attention and what we fight for in terms of negative and positive things. By focusing on these things we may be able to identify some elements of our story.

There are other stories we construct on a larger scale to do with our families, cultures, countries and the world. It is important to bear in mind that the blueprint of the stories comes back to our early hidden memories. These are the building blocks of our beliefs. I would like to emphasize the fact that many of us are not even aware of the emotional elements of our story. We may know and understand our story intellectually, and think we are dealing with it, but emotionally it has a hold on us because what we *know* we do not necessarily allow ourselves to *feel*. In other words, there is a disconnection between them. We often do not feel what we know.

> '*A man is always a storyteller; he tries to see his life as if he were telling it. But one has to choose: to live or to tell.*'
> JEAN-PAUL SARTRE (1905–80), FRENCH PHILOSOPHER, PLAYWRIGHT AND NOVELIST

# PART II
## The Healing Process

# INTRODUCTION

## The search for freedom

Part I sheds light on *how to* understand the limitations that we create for ourselves, by our unsuccessful attempts to protect ourselves, and the hidden choices directing our decisions and our selection of partners or professions. These limitations take away our power in every action and decision in our lives.

In Part II we will explore how to live life more consciously from your essence, from your conscious mind, and how to gain that consciousness and be compassionate toward others and yourself.

Learning to live from your essence is the longest journey, yet with the shortest distance, and is about living your feelings in the *now*: living from your immediate conscious actions and not from your reactions from your subconscious.

The words *how to* might imply that there is a method to achieving happiness and freedom, but I must emphasize that there is no method, formula, plan or technique you can employ to tackle life. Formulas or methods only add to its complexity and lead to denying the mystery of simply *being*. There is no road map to being free and there is no rulebook for life. All so-called methods are based on problems, which supposedly need to be solved at the end of it. But nothing has an end to it. Who we are in our souls has no beginning or ending. Our essence just is. It is total presence in the moment. It is all about awareness in the present moment, which brings healing immediately because it has no past to fix, no future to anticipate or even any present to understand – no beginning and no end.

It may not be possible to find peace and freedom through any organization, teachings, methods, techniques or knowledge because the practice of any teaching or system can lead to conformity, resistance, denial and then, perhaps, adjustment. Our energy is wasted on seeking a way out rather than taking responsibility for finding our freedom. The most inspiring people in the world had no system for what to do. There was no therapist for Sigmund Freud. Mahatma Gandhi didn't have a *method* for liberating India. In fact, when he was asked to give a message to the world about what they should do and how they should live, he said, 'My life is my message.' In the same way, explore the message of this book by living consciously.

Even though I will share with you some strategies to apply in your life, my emphasis is on enhancing your insights to support your journey to be in your essence, to be present with what is and accept it. Insights will be established through your relationships, through observing your own reactions and maintaining your conscious focus, rather than through intellectual theories, ideas and methods.

*'To know oneself is to study oneself in action with another person.'*
BRUCE LEE (1940–73), CHINESE MARTIAL ARTIST AND ACTOR

# Understanding alone is not enough

The world today is becoming more and more orientated to a life led by our intellect rather than by emotion or feeling and we may be in danger of going to the other extreme and losing our heart. The intellect tells us how we *ought* to be, how we *ought* to feel and even how we *ought* to love. While therapy is a very supportive and effective way of helping people, we pay money for it in order to be able to express our feelings in the hope it can somehow compensate for the parent we may not have had providing us with love and attention. We have even tried to know intellectually how to become religious, how to love and how to become spiritual. The intellect suggests that in order to become spiritual, you must go to a spiritual place and live among spiritual people. In order to become loving, we have to take courses or read books or listen to teachers. We recognize the need for more compassion and the intellect may suggest we can learn this by buying a book on the subject, while loving ourselves is not a scientific endeavour.

We try to learn how to live through information, courses, religion and therapy. These things, although they are no doubt very helpful, are also attempts to find constancy in an inconsistent and spontaneous world. We seek consistency because it is safe and familiar. When we see inconsistencies in life, we feel unsafe. Life is actually in a constant state of inconsistency and flux, but we keep on doing the same things we have always done in the past because this is what is familiar and we know but it is not truly what is in our *now*.

*We have become slaves to our conclusions.*

Life is a reality to be experienced and not a project or problem to be solved intellectually. Our intellect needs conclusions and ideas but we have become slaves to them. Our intellect needs to analyze and see how things have come together, but in the process we run the risk of not seeing beyond systems, methods or formulas. To be conscious is the journey toward appreciating our lives now and finding our essence. Although even the words 'finding our essence' can be misleading because we are already in our essence and we cannot search outside for it because it is here and now; it is in the immediate moment of consciousness. Let us explore this most unique journey that has no destination, in order to appreciate our lives now and live from our essence consciously.

# CHAPTER 1
# THINKING AND FEELING

*All our feelings lie behind the masks we wear, so it is
better to feel our thinking than think our feelings.*

## Our capacity to feel

Our *Protector*, as discussed in Part I, is composed of layers
of defensive patterns and adaptations, which keep our
feelings at a distance, depriving us of being open in our
feelings toward others. Understanding alone cannot stop
these disrupted connections from occurring because they
are neurological, biological connections in the brain that
cannot change, which is why it is so difficult to change.

Feelings are the central focus of Part II, as they are also
the starting point from which you can be in your essence.
This is simply because our feelings are the first connection
we have to life before thinking. If you observe young children
you will see that they react to life with emotions and feelings
first, and then later learn to speak and rationalize. In the
world of adults this is reversed, as adults usually express
their rational views first and then later show their emotions.
But our original means of communication is through our
feelings. Some of them can be misunderstood if we *think*

them but not if we *feel* them. These emotions and feelings are the foundation of what it is to be human.

The images of everything that happened to us in life are stored in our mind and these mental patterns provoke us to make presumptions about who we think we are. There are many physical sensations and feelings, however, which also came into existence at the same time – from the beginning of our lives – and which also make up who we think we are. The challenge for us is to feel these feelings and see how they have survived the journey from complete *un*awareness through to consciousness and to ascertain how our feelings have affected us. Part of this understanding is to discover what we have missed feeling and how to understand or make sense of our feelings, what became invisible along the way and what has survived and entered our conscious awareness.

When we were children, we didn't have the intellect or understanding to deal with strong emotions, such as feelings of fear and abandonment; we did not have the adult perspective of seeing how the world operates. But we can acknowledge our feelings now and understand why and how they came about.

Healing is not only about increasing knowledge; it is also about our capacity to feel. Feelings are our instinctive ability to respond to stimuli in the environment. The *Protector* is our automatic reaction to suppress our unresolved feelings of pain and fear. The resistance it puts up, however, becomes more painful than the original sensation and this resistance to pain can turn into suffering.

> 'The resistance to the unpleasant situation
> is the root of suffering.'
> RAM DASS

The dynamic of pain behind our fear is very important. Fear is a warning signal of pain that tells us we are in danger and therefore any feelings of pain must be avoided. Many people try not to feel pain by going overboard and trying to do many things. For example, in order to avoid being lonely or being rejected, they have as many friends as possible or are very busy and work very hard. Unfortunately, they only address the symptoms of pain and such attempts only reinforce its power by trying to avoid the original feeling of the early separation and hurt. Even a desire to heal is a desire to avoid pain.

This book is an insight into understanding your *Protector's* dynamic that has unfolded in the attempts to resist feeling pain and fear. On the other hand, intellectual understanding can serve as just another avoidance technique. This is why experiential education in a group setting can be a very good place to move the information from the intellectual domain into the feeling domain – an area which most of us avoid. When we undertake any form of therapy, read self-help books and listen to lectures on self-improvement or personal development (even reading this book right now), we tend to use our developed intellect – that is, our present brain development – in order to heal older, deeper emotional feelings.

I am not against any therapeutic approach, but many approaches, especially cognitive, aim to give us strategies for coping with painful situations. Cognitive approaches are very powerful and can have a real effect on how we manage our reactive responses. Also, using strategies can be helpful in overcoming certain barriers, but they are still in the intellect domain, which is subject to conclusions and assumptions that have been accumulated over the years of images from experiences. Our true being (our essence) is beyond that; it is here and now in the split second before our *Protector* hijacks us and takes charge of our behaviour.

The sophisticated intellect of the brain is fascinated with words and explanations, ideas and concepts, but it does not have the capability to deal with old, unprocessed and unexplained imprinted feelings, experiences and memories. Moreover, this is the biggest challenge we face in our self-development work, because these approaches can give you a short-term fix but no long-term solution.

## There is no set of instructions for being in your essence

This book is not about what to do next in order to be free because there is no set of instructions for attaining freedom. There are many ways in which we deal with the inconsistencies of life's challenges; invoking our *Protector* is just one of them. Other ways include religion, therapy, reading and also through deep loving and compassion.

Some people don't do anything at all. The ways listed above can all be means by which the brain can attain freedom, but our essence has no set of instructions to follow. If we should find a system or formula, we will eventually become trapped by it. Finding our essence is all about remembering who we are within the dimensions of our consciousness.

Only relationships shape your reactions in the form of the *Protector*. Therefore your *Protector* is the teacher that will lead you to your freedom and your essence. This journey to your essence has no definitive distance; it unfolds in your relationships that are a mirror of yourself. We make sense of who we are through relationships, and we learn how to love through relationships; we also learn how to be unloved through relationships.

Some people have managed to heal themselves by finding healing relationships that support them. Some people don't manage to find such relationships. Others find a way to heal their pain by serving the world and making a huge contribution to it. Some decide to become therapists, healers, doctors or religious leaders. I would say this is all perfect as long as we are conscious of what we are doing to heal ourselves. Otherwise, the way we try to heal ourselves can become another mask, protecting us in order to be safe.

Many people try following sets of instructions, including religion, politics, therapeutic techniques, associations, groups, cults, rituals and taking up a cause. The result of this, however, is that we are still seeking because we are looking outside ourselves for the answers and thus we become slaves to our concepts and beliefs. There is no manual on how to live life or bring up our children. No one can change your life but you. No one can get inside your brain and show you what to do. Others can only show you what they feel works for them.

We need to be wary of anyone who wants to teach us methods by which to live. In addition, we must be careful not to teach ours to other people. In fact, I would suggest to you that people who have a desire to help others are actually using them to heal their unfelt pain. Some parents do this to their children, too.

*'We must seek the company of those who are looking for the truth and avoid those who have found it.'*
DEEPAK CHOPRA, SPIRITUAL TEACHER AND AUTHOR

The way to healing is to *be* the statement of your essence. People don't care how much we can teach them, but they *feel* how much love we have.

This is a very individual journey and will have an impact on your life and others around you, without your having to teach anyone anything. If enough people in the world were fully conscious, the world would change by itself. You need to read the information in this book and let it be absorbed by your heart, so that it can support you in working on yourself. It is all about deep self-observation in order to bring about a realization of the appreciation of self-change. It is about awakening your inner and outer worlds. Most challenges arise because we don't take responsibility for how our inner and outer worlds interact and affect our lives. It provokes the very interesting question as to whether we are living our lives from within, reacting to the world outside, or trying to find the balance between the two. Or just being conscious and allowing with trust everything to happen by itself.

> *'Your vision will become clear when you look into*
> *your heart. Who looks outside, dreams;*
> *who looks inside, awakens.'*
> CARL JUNG (1875–1961),
> SWISS PSYCHIATRIST AND INFLUENTIAL THINKER

## Who are you?

How do you know who you are? If your brain processes all the mechanical activity that is dependent on outside circumstances, then who is making all the decisions? Who is behind all that? Who are you exactly?

The brain is like a computer with short-term and long-term memory. But who is operating the computer? Who is making the decisions? Just pause a moment as you consider this and you may see the answer to everything now without trying.

We know how decisions are processed and executed, but where is the person who is doing all this? We have sophisticated machines, which can show us all our brain activities and processes, but they cannot show who initiates these activities. Can I ask you: who is reading this book? This is it. You are reading this information and this information will help support your brain, which allows your essence to manifest.

We experience our consciousness in the world despite the fact that we can't identify one single area in the brain that is capable of performing the function of directing our intentions or of making decisions. Decision-making is heavily influenced by our memories and past protections. Our conscious decisions are very much clouded by our unconscious decisions all the time due to how our memories shaped the construction of who we think we are.

But we must be more than who we think we are; there is a real dimension behind it all that is our consciousness *now*. It has no past or future, or even present, no beginning and no end to our essence. Our essence is the part of us that is real and is not changed by outside circumstances. It uses the brain to communicate and function in this world but it doesn't depend on memory. It doesn't depend on blame or praise, love or hate. It may not reside in the brain at all since our brain may be only a tool through which our essence uses to manifest, and it is the tool we use to function effectively in this world. The brain is designed to protect, judge, assess, adapt and manoeuvre in order for us to survive. It is like an anticipation machine, balancing the world for us. This means that if we don't live from our essence we are in danger of becoming a reactive response mechanism.

Our culture, family and education shape our brains, and we could say that it is the mechanical part of us that is affected by outside circumstances and organized by blame or praise. It functions with and through our memories and beliefs. But it is not who we are. It is only one dimension of us. The other dimension is our essence.

Both dimensions interact with each other in everything we do in life: our essence needs our brain to express itself in this world. We live from our essence and communicate through our brain. Therefore a clear brain helps us to live fully in our essence. This is why we need to examine and explore our personality and get to know our *Protector*, which might distort our clarity. We need to be aware of the *Protector* when it is protecting us and witness how the *Protector* functions as a mechanism of the brain, inasmuch as it is a cause-and-effect dynamic. Its purpose is to shield us from pain and hurt. Our essence, however, comes from another level of consciousness, where everything is perfect just the way it is. Our brain may not be able to understand this because it is not designed this way; it is designed to protect us and we need to accept that, too. It is not a bad thing but if we let it control us, it may not support who we are.

The journey to be in our essence is a very long one, even though it is a very short distance, because we are crossing planes of consciousness from the mechanical brain (who we think we are) to another dimension to our essence (who we actually are). If we can just grasp the meaning of these words, our entire world will be transformed. Who we are is everyone; you are the world. When we hate someone, we hate ourselves and we feel it.

The question here is, how can the brain, which has formed such unconscious coping strategies and defence mechanisms, change its own conditioning? Can our thoughts rise above themselves in order to solve the strategies they created in the first place? In other words, can the brain change the brain? How can that be done?

It is important to remember that problems can't be resolved, because they are in fact shadows of feelings within the mindset from which they were originally created. Therefore, the answer must lie outside our beliefs and perceptions.

## The essence process: a journey with no destination

In Part I we saw how our beliefs are the biggest challenge we face in life. Since we absorb beliefs from our family and culture, especially when very young, we have produced everything we have now in our lives. Our personality has been developed from others through our education, beliefs and past experiences. Others trained us how to live and how to react and interact, and, in so doing, we developed our *Protector*. This part of us, which constructs our personal identity, continues to be helped or hindered by the demands of *others*. We also explored how and where in the brain the activities of the *Protector* show themselves and the next step is to get more in touch with your essence.

Your essence is neutral in the moment that it allows you to witness the good and the bad, and the right and the wrong in everything that has happened to you in the past in its complete vastness and without judgement.

So far we have established the price we pay for living in the shadow of the *Protector*. The purpose of our journey is not to eliminate this protective personality – because if we try to do this we will be setting up another protective personality – but to see it as it is. So our *Protector* is, in fact, leading us to our essence by teaching us how to see it as it is. We can only see it by having compassion for ourselves.

## The journey

Our journey and purpose here is to raise our consciousness enough to have compassion in our hearts for our *Protector*. The paradox here is *awareness*, because if our *Protector* knows itself, then there is no longer any need for it. This can only happen by raising our awareness and consciousness so that we are at peace with all the conflicts within us and are able to see others as they really are, not as those who would hurt us.

Seeking our essence is not even a journey because in the very act of seeking we would yet again be attempting to escape from our pain and trying to be enlightened, which is another aspect of our *Protector*. It is a question of opening our hearts in order to be at peace and accept the way things are in others, in our past and ourselves, and to be able to say 'yes' to it all. This requires tremendous work on oneself because these are the obstacles that block our essence.

## How the journey starts

It is fascinating to observe how the child's attempts to 'make things better' actually become symptoms of the *Protector*. Our unsuccessful attempts in childhood at protecting ourselves from danger are reactions, which subsequently manifest in our adult life. Furthermore, these childlike reactions aimed at protecting ourselves from suffering can result in addictions, neuroses, self-absorbed or narcissistic disorders, destructive behaviours and so forth. In fact, trying to avoid pain and suffering only leads to greater pain and suffering. We need to cultivate the awareness that we can meet our pain. As we do so, we will also finally become aware that who we are has nothing to do with pain and suffering.

## The journey continues

Our *Protector* develops by attracting experiences, which eventually reinforce the memories left behind by the original experience. Over the years, this personality grows beyond its original role of protecting us; it acquires a life of its own and becomes a powerful network of unconscious attitudes and patterns of behaviour, thus dominating almost every aspect of our lives. The consequence of this growth results in behaviours that are contrary to who we are and to our true intentions. We are therefore left with the distressing contradiction of trying to achieve our true intentions, but failing to do so.

## The journey ends with love

This protective behaviour is a voice speaking to you, saying, 'I want to make you safe from abandonment.' The voice of love, by contrast, says, 'I am safe even though my heart is breaking.' Our *Protector* seeks our safety by protecting us from danger. It does this because it desperately needs you to feel love. When you *are* love, however, there is no longer any need to protect yourself from danger because you already have the love you need and no longer need to seek it out. Just as you read this, remember a moment when you were falling in love. There is no fear or pain whatsoever; all that comes later when you start wondering whether the person loves you or not, and whether they will stay with you or not. This is the invitation to the *Protector* to start working to try to keep the love, but unfortunately it pushes the love away because the person who loves you loves you for who you are and not for who you are trying to be in order to make them love you.

# CHAPTER 2
# AWARENESS OF LIMITATION + COMPASSION FOR ONESELF = TRANSFORMATION

*The one who judges you the most, loves you the most and has the most compassion for you is YOU.*

## Awareness is our greatest healer

The experiences that have happened to us in the past cannot be changed. The only chance we have is to deal with our past, but in order to regain our strength we need to see things as they are.

Being able to understand what happened to us and to face the reality of unbearable events will result in even more pain, but it is the only way to freedom. I recall the poet William Blake's words when he said, 'Human beings cannot tolerate too much reality.'

In these words lies the essence of our healing, the meaning being that we should tolerate reality not out of fear or submission, but out of love and compassion. It is all about agreeing with what is. We cannot see things as they are unless we know that what we have seen in the past came out of an old perspective that wasn't real. We can never be free until we see what we have stored in our memory and what we were not aware of; we can never be free until we know what we are free from – that is, our unconscious past memories. If you do not realize that you are in prison, you will never escape.

This is our starting point. To be aware of our brain's survival strategy is to be aware of our *Protector*.

Do not be afraid of your past, as the key to healing is the awareness that your past is past. All your past actions will have been determined by the avoidance of a danger, which doesn't exist any more.

One of the real challenges and tragedies in this life is when some children, who have been traumatized, don't even know that they have been traumatized. This is because they have got used to things being this way and think it is normal. On the one hand, they have managed to develop some kind of resilience, while on the other, the brain still has the painful memory and fear reaction to those painful experiences. When these children grow up, they may well say that the past is the past and be stronger for their experiences. Although they may not be able to even give love in a relationship, because they don't have the experience of receiving it; we can't give anything that we don't have.

These people are in so much pain that they may develop a stronger *Protector* in order to cope and may live their lives in denial of the pain of being unloved. They may also hide this pain of being unloved by desiring to help others. This pain was not consciously felt when they were children, but they developed a way of coping with it in a multitude of ways. If they subsequently have the experience of being rejected in a relationship or of losing someone, they may be triggered into accessing their pain. In so doing, they could well have a breakdown. At the moment of extreme pain, however, the *Protector* starts to break down and they may identify the falsehood of it. They thought this character was who they were but in this moment of awareness, freedom follows as they realize that it wasn't who they were at all. They have identified the *Protector* as being false – and what is left is their essence.

The healing in this area requires extraordinary work on oneself to become aware of what has happened and how it has affected us. The point here is that in order to accept the past, we need to see it, feel the pain first and recognize that we have been deeply hurt; otherwise we will find ourselves stuck in an illusory world in which we tell ourselves, 'No one hurt me; no one can hurt me and I am OK.' Or, the opposite, which is to play a game using our past as punishment and a reason for our failure.

## Exercise for the reader

*Let us begin with an awareness exercise to help you to uncover some aspects of your* Protector. *Find someone to ask you the questions below. It is important that you don't do this exercise alone. If you do this exercise with more than one other person then so much the better, because interactions in relationships are very important. Start with any behaviour that limits you, for example always being late for appointments, feeling sad or emotional, or talking too much. Then withdraw, hold back and answer the questions spontaneously, without trying to work out or choose an answer – just let the answers flow and see what comes up. When you reach the end of the questions, start again with another limiting behaviour. After you finish, ask the person or people with whom you are doing the exercise to reflect back on what you've said. Listen carefully to what they say. After their feedback, don't respond to it. Spend a quiet moment with yourself and make no effort whatsoever.*

1 *What is a behaviour that limits you? Describe an example.*

2 *Describe the negative image that you have about yourself when behaving in this way.*

3 *Describe any sensations that you experience as you talk about this negative image.*

4 *From what does the behaviour seem to protect you?*

5 *What is your fear?*

6 *Recall any images or experiences from the past that connect you to this fear.*

7 *Is this fear real now?*

*Reflect on this exercise and just allow all the information to sink into your awareness without any effort to change anything. Awareness is just being in the moment; it is a cure in itself.*

The challenge for us is that when we become aware, we tend to struggle more and this struggle comes from trying to make sense of or analyze our limitations. If we don't like what we see, we judge, analyze or try to change ourselves. As soon as we do that, we immediately lose the awareness and apply more effort to change. The moment of awareness doesn't require any effort whatsoever. Any efforts we make will entail a struggle to change *what is* to *what is not*. Our conditioning will automatically make us feel that this is bad, or that we should change and be good. We are so used to saying 'should' that we impose judgement and criticism upon ourselves.

One of the ways we learn to survive is by competition and trying to be better at what we do in order to succeed. The drive within us is to be someone successful and we try to avoid failure. Therefore life becomes a battle between *good* and *bad*, as we were once punished for doing *bad* things and rewarded when we did *good* things. Life, therefore, became a duality divided between *good* and *bad*, according to our conditioning.

This isn't about the agreements that society makes about paying taxes and law and order; it is about our conditioned responses and how socializations have an effect on the way we react to our *Protector*.

> *'Out beyond the ideas of wrongdoing or right doing,*
> *there is a field. I will meet you there.'*
> RUMI (1207–73), PERSIAN POET AND MYSTIC

# I must change

Without hesitation or fear, we need to approach the realization of the existence of our limitations, without any desire whatsoever to change it. If we say to ourselves, 'I must change,' we will be confirming to ourselves that something is wrong with us and, as a result, we will fight our limitations instead of peacefully realizing what they are. We don't want to be in the position of fighting a war with another war in order to find peace in our hearts.

We are already perfect. Our limitations don't change who we already are. The desire and fight for perfection create more needless anxiety and may result in attracting further obstacles, which engender further limitations and so on. If we fight anything, it will fight us back and we will become like those whom we fight. In other words, as soon as we fight, we lose.

Life is not a conflict and a problem that needs to be solved; it as a reality to be experienced with limitless possibilities. The longer we struggle against life or anything we don't want to see, the more we reinforce its reality. Therefore, it is better to step into reality and experience it willingly rather than fight it.

Step into the reality of your protective behaviours. The true transformation occurs when you have compassion for yourself, instead of wishing to change, because any attempts to change, any attempts to get rid of unwanted behaviours, immediately push you out of awareness.

For example, the moment you grasp an aspect of your *Protector*, you need to surrender completely to the feeling of the behaviour without expressing or suppressing it.

Such direct experience often reveals a deeper emotion and connection to life, and awakens in you the ability to feel everything from the heart.

We don't want to face the fact that we are afraid; therefore we will pursue security with the resultant fear of not being secure. Only within your heart and essence can you be open to every situation in life that comes your way and say, 'Yes' to how things were and are now. This requires a deep love for yourself in order to learn and keep on learning. The *Protector* fights for its life in order to survive at all costs, so as soon as you become aware of your reactions and see your limitations, you are well on your way to self-awareness. The healing can be in getting in touch with the sensations that preceded the reaction.

The *Protector* impels us to change ourselves in some way, in order to survive. It wants to emphasize all those things that we perceive as failures or threats and what we don't like about ourselves. The moment we come across something we are not happy with, we might say, 'What do I do about it?' At that point, we immediately lose our awareness.

Preconceptions and obsessions with improving yourself will only take you away from the moment to a future hope that whatever has upset you will not happen again. Wishing and hoping to change comes from a sense of desperation. The focus is on hoping for change, but more desperation and hopelessness are what we end up creating instead. Most human problems arise from the expectations we have of change and our struggle to be 'better'. This is the conflict. If you push against something, it will defy you, and you will end up with more separation.

# Risk

In order to heal and feel real love, we must be willing to risk the experience of first being unloved. This means risking feeling the primary pain of rejection. To gain control you must first lose control.

It is a bit like walking if each time you took a step you lost another. When we were young and confronted with anxiety and distressing situations, we needed the comfort and reassurance of our parents or caregivers. Those who don't receive this try to adapt and use self-control in order to survive. In some severe cases, the parent is angry and responds to the child in an aggressive way, which adds more pain and fear, resulting in the child making further attempts to adapt. These attempts carry a shadow of the fear of abandonment from the very person who should be protecting them from this fear. This has a devastating effect upon the child and lasts for a lifetime.

This person will develop a *Protector* that is very much afraid of being abandoned by the person they love. They are afraid of aggression, intimidation and also of being rejected. Therefore, when they grow up, his or her *Protector* will be very much on the alert in personal relationships. They may shrink in arguments or confrontations and avoid conflicts and feel unsafe with the relationship. They can never take risks in confronting the people with whom they have relationships and find it hard to trust. This develops into a pattern, which repeats itself in every relationship, business, marriage or partnership of any kind. In the desperate attempt to protect the self, this person withdraws emotionally on the outside but carries distress and anxiety on the inside. Consequently, they may appear inauthentic in relationships.

Other people may develop in exactly the opposite way and react very quickly, being angry on the outside and terrified on the inside. The decisions from the *Protector* can mirror the parent, so we copy our parents' strategy at the same time as we develop our own protection from the way they have treated us.

If you have children, you can learn a lot about yourself by watching how they protect themselves from fear. You will see what you do yourself and, having observed this, the last thing you should do is correct your children. Although you may do this because you have the desire to heal yourself and they remind you of how you have protected yourself.

True healing takes place by taking risks with expressing emotions. Let your emotions out, obviously without a huge drama, but be very conscious of what it feels like when we express them. If the person to whom you express them is supportive and understanding, then you will begin to heal these reactions. If the person isn't understanding and rejects you, this will provide feedback for you concerning the other person and it may be that you need to evaluate whether this person is the one to support you in your journey to be free. Let them also express their reactions and be sympathetic to their response, even if they don't agree with you. This will allow you to be even more aware of yourself, as you will find that this person also represents parts of yourself. This is worth taking a risk for.

# Judging and forgiving

We have grown up conditioned to compare ourselves with others by constantly judging whether we are better or worse than them. As this leads us to judge ourselves even more, the person who judges us most is ourselves. At the moment of self-judgement, when we separate ourselves from who we really are, we become both judge and victim. When we judge others or ourselves, we are not in the present moment and, moreover, we live in negative feelings and attract more negativity to our lives. Being non-judgemental allows you to see yourself with compassion.

*When the moment comes and you stop comparing yourself to others, it is a signal that you are awakening your essence that is beyond judgement or comparing.*

Compassion is missing in our lives, especially now more than ever. One of the unconscious reasons that people see a therapist is to be in the presence of someone while at the same time not feeling as if they are being judged or shamed. We are now in a culture where we have to pay money for compassion. What we are really missing is the unconditional love we had when we were very young and we strive to find it again by appealing to our *Protector*.

In reality, it may not be possible to live in the world without judging anyone, but if we judge people, we still can choose whether to hold on to that judgement and for how long. It is our responsibility how we approach judgement and what we do with it. Because we are often unable to do this for ourselves, we go to professionals who are trained to be non-judgemental and neutral.

## Exercise for the reader

*Here is an exercise to help you to identify how you judge and forgive yourself. Find a person and ask him or her to ask you the following questions. There is no need to think about the answer – just allow them to unfold. Repeat the questions and answers several times until you identify the motivation behind your protective actions.*

1 *What do you want to achieve in your life?*

2 *What is your fear if you fail to achieve it?*

3 *What do you judge yourself for not achieving?*

4 *Can you recall any triggering event that provokes your fear and self-judgement?*

5 *How do you hide your fear and self-judgement? How do you pretend that you are OK?*

6 *Complete this statement: I forgive myself for judging myself for…*

The *Protector* is the dynamic of hiding your fear and self-judgement and so by becoming aware of how we try to hide our fear, the *Protector's* strategies will reveal themselves to us.

*'The idea is very much like a sculpture… not to add on but hack away the unessential so that the truth will be revealed unobstructed.'*
BRUCE LEE

# CHAPTER 3
# THE OBSERVER AND
# THE OBSERVED

*The* Protector *is a mask concealing who you are with who you think you are. When we wear the mask for too long, we no longer know the difference between the mask and ourselves.*

## Observing your reactions

When we feel bad about ourselves, we automatically try to get rid of our irritation by either blaming ourselves or blaming others for being the cause of it. The reason we blame others is that we can't stand other people having the same faults as us. This is the reason some people have a conflicting relationship with their parents. So, when we can't stand some aspect of ourselves, our *Protector* responds by attacking or judging other people who have the very thing we don't like about ourselves. We judge them or try to make them change according to our standards, which we ourselves cannot fulfil. The *Protector* can also cover up our self-dislike by attempting to nurture others, for example by giving them the things that we don't have (and at the same time rejecting ourselves for not having them).

At this stage we are not living from our essence; we are living from our *Protector*.

The question is how to see the *Protector* and reactions as they are just by simply observing our reactions to our limitations? This will allow us to see the *Protector* protecting us in action and such observations will shift us to *watching* rather than being hijacked by the *Protector*. This is a huge step to take in developing ourselves. If we can observe then we will see that we are controlled by our reactions in every moment and instead of them controlling us, we can begin to control them until they are no longer contributing to our false self-image. The key here is to watch with compassion and not with judgement; judgement is one of the *Protector's* qualities, not ours.

As you can see, in order to free yourself from self-judgement, observation will allow you to be free of the reactions of your protective personality. This will require a full appreciation of who you are and the reasons why you react as you do. In so doing you should not apply pity but compassion for yourself. We must never fight, ignore or reject our pain, as this is what makes us alive and awakens us to our reactions.

Take a pause for a moment and take a deep breath before you plunge into making judgements. It is only then that you can see your protective behaviour as a ripple on the surface of a lake. Underneath the surface there is fear, anger, and even rage and pain but we will clearly see our reactions to what we don't want to see in ourselves, and how our defences become like constantly changing masks which we wear in trying to adapt to every situation. In this way you will see that your strategies are childlike attempts to cope with the world around you and that while you continue to employ these strategies, you will continue to forget who you really are – your essence.

It is a *split second* between exposure to a stimulus and our reaction, and it takes a long time to acquire the skill to become aware within this minuscule time frame. It takes a lot of work on oneself to be conscious of these moments. This requires us to live consciously. In these split seconds we are acting from our essence. Some people call it living from the heart when we act from who we are and do not behave in ways that satisfy people's expectations of us. There are moments in our lives when we have done that many times and there was no thinking, no conclusions or even *trying* to live from the heart.

I would say that everything in life can be acquired by observation and repetition, and we can also develop the skill to be centred and focused on who we are. Our being is very much connected to and interactive with our environment, constantly guarding and protecting, dependent entirely on how we react to outside influences. The outside world's environment depends upon a series of either good or bad events, according to our beliefs and conditioning. These challenging events are always going to be there. What we need to worry about is not what happened in the inconsistent environment but how we react to it.

Reactions allow outside circumstances to take control. The brain becomes immersed and we lose essence; thus, we lose self-control. Our reactions can add more worry and so we end up making more lists, creating things to do in order to avoid pain and setting up tasks and projects. We become slaves to the outside environment because all the things we are creating come from the brain, which is completely dominated by the *Protector*. Thus, we can lose our sense of self and, rather than being who we are, we become who we think we are, which is our *Protector*.

We need to remember ourselves and not get sucked into what the environment demands of us. We must move on from valuing what we do, to valuing who we are.

It is important to bring our awareness to how we adapt to the external environment and see what we are doing in order to achieve love, attention or approval. This awareness will give us time to process and feel the experiences we are experiencing rather than reacting and struggling to find unsuccessful solutions.

We need to pause and feel the need and understand what this need is about; to feel the pain of not having our needs met, to feel sad and to know what we are sad about. When we feel sadness or painful experiences from the past, we allow the memory back into our consciousness and we must stop and just *feel* it. If we avoid doing this we will end up running away faster towards our *Protector*. We also need to learn to be with our feelings rather than suppressing them which is what the *Protector* does all the time. If we succeed in this we will begin a maturing process.

## Observe your interactions

The best indicators of your *Protector* are found in your interactions within relationships because our brains are designed to react in order for us to survive and our work begins by exploring these interactions. In isolation, we may not identify what we do as we are not responding so much to stimuli.

These interactions show us that, while we have

unsettled and unfinished business to complete, it is almost impossible to escape from our hidden memories. Anyone in our present-day relationships who causes us to react in a certain way can be our teacher. We can learn from these people because they often represent past experiences that trigger our hidden memory, as in the case of people in authority, for example. We may find we react to them in the same way we did in the past. In paying close attention to our reactions to people and relationships we can see them as opportunities to bring more awareness into our lives about how our past memories influence us. We especially need to pay more attention to anything that confuses or challenges us in our communications with others, as well as what might confuse or challenge them about us. If people are confused about our communication with them, this in itself is feedback for us about how our *Protector* communicates. Confusion and lack of clarity are a strategy of the *Protector*, too. Speaking from our essence consciously in the present moment has unquestionable clarity. My observations when I work with groups are that when people speak from that place everyone listens immediately because they are authentic and are communicating from their real being. When people avoid doing this or play games in their communication, they lose the attention of their listeners very quickly.

Communication is key here. Recall your dialogue when you speak to people and if you can observe yourself speaking, you will find that sometimes your communication may not match your intention or inner voice. This often happens when preparing to speak. When we deliver our words, if we are not conscious in the moment (in our essence) we can end up saying things we do not mean in any conversation; we lose focus and are hijacked by our *Protector*.

Each day-to-day human interaction can unravel considerable information about the existence of our reactions to hidden memories. Even gestures, facial expressions and body movements, when you find yourself in challenging situations, can give you valuable insights.

This will help you to become aware of all the aspects of your protective behaviour, as these come not only from the brain, but also from the entire body.

What often happens during a conversation with someone is that we can lose being conscious of who we are and get hijacked by our reactions. If you can observe the other person's expressions and also observe your own reactions, you will begin to communicate from your essence.

Observing our reactions to whatever is happening, without judging either the good or the bad in them, calls for an extraordinarily sharp attention, even to being watchful of the desire not to judge, as this is also another manifestation of our desire to be *good*. An extraordinarily sharp mind can see the fine line between our unconscious response and our conscious reflection. When we see our *Protector* in this way, without any reaction whatsoever, then it can cease in its unsuccessful attempts to enact a survival strategy. This kind of observation is like meditation, transcending the *good* or *bad*, *better* or *worse*.

## Observe your reality

What is reality? How do you know this is reality? We seem to live using symbols to define reality, and we often confuse them with actual reality. For instance, your name is a symbol; it is not you. Money is a symbol of being rich. Ideas are also symbols that separate us from reality, as are the images we have about ourselves. Reality is actually so simple; it is you reading this book right now – nothing else. When we are under stress, however, our bodies inhibit conscious reflection and, in order to cope, promote our *Protector*. In this mode, we are less able to see reality, as we see only our own made-up reality. We are caught in a stress response to situations, which creates a perspective of reality to which we respond. When we look back later, we often wonder why we reacted the way we did.

> *'The most obvious is that which is never seen until someone expresses it simply.'*
> KHALIL GIBRAN (1883–1991), LEBANESE-AMERICAN
> PHILOSOPHER AND POET

Unfortunately, many of us live in a world where stress is increasingly part of our everyday lives. We worry about money, relationships and our health. Our environment is full of stress and many of us don't have access to traditional modes of support – family and community – as we move toward individualism. The pressure is shifting from the group to the individual; thus, our environment provokes fear and, of course, our false perceptions are increasing more and more. Consequently, our *Protector* also increases in strength and presence.

## Observe your perceptions

Our brain has models of reality and then continuously adapts them and changes to cope with the environment through the information that reaches our senses. It is in a state of change all the time. We are at risk of perceiving the real world from the brain's old model of the world, as provided from past intense experiences. We may be in danger of seeing a false world because we are our beliefs and fantasies from predisposing memory in the brain.

How do we know if our brain model is true or not? We know by whether or not we get the results we want. The model reveals itself when we communicate with others and then we can see clearly that other models can be different from ours. Everything we experience hinges on the memory we give it. By paying attention to how effective our communication is, we will also see that we live in a reality of our own making and create our own world. It is very difficult to be convinced otherwise, and we fight for our reality: as it says in Richard Bach's novel *Illusions: The Adventures of a Reluctant Messiah*, 'Argue with your own limitations as they are certainly yours.'

If you are unhappy with your perception of reality, you can change it first by observing how you experience the world and then by beginning to see the world in a different way, as you want to see it.

## Observe your image

Each of us makes up an image of ourselves based on our protective behaviour. This is, however, the very thing we don't like about ourselves, because we have another image of how we *should* be. When we see our limitations, we tell ourselves *I should be this* or *I should not be that*. Now we have one image built out of our protective behaviour and another one built out of our reaction to that protective behaviour. In this battle between *I am like this, but I should be like that* we forget our essence. This is because we are afraid of seeing our imperfections and defend the image of being perfect. From this point, the protective behaviour drives us into pretending to be perfect. The problem arises when we forget how we *should be* and make mistakes, such as telling lies, for instance. Then we find ourselves in contradiction with our standards of perfection and we hate and fight ourselves even more. The unrealistic self-image is shattered.

## Observe the unknown

As we become attached to our *Protector*, we become self-absorbed and self-deceptive about our real selves. Our *Protector* has become *the known*; this is who we think we are. To live without the *Protector* is the unknown. We don't know any different mode and the thought of living without our *Protector* creates a sense of fear of the unknown. The unknown, however, is beyond our fear, our emptiness and our suffering. It is beyond our beliefs that we are not loved.

The unknown is our real self but we cling on to our suffering and give up on the happiness we want, because we don't want to let go of what is known and our familiar reactions to past experiences and memories.

*When you let go of who you think you are,*
*you become who you are.*

Our biggest fear, however, should be *the known*, because if we let go of what we know, we will find freedom. Most people have a fear of the unknown, but this is maybe yet another belief that most humans have absorbed. We could change this around and tell ourselves that our biggest fear is not of the unknown, but the known. The reason we could choose to do this is because, although what we have known in the past has been painful, the unknown is full of possibilities.

## Observe your desire for perfection

We seem to be trained to learn by contrast. When we see how our *Protector* acts in a bad way, we see ourselves as *bad*. We try to be *good*, but according to the high standards we have set for ourselves. In this way our lives have become a battle between *good* and *bad* and, as a result, we see other people as either *good* or *bad*, too. We have lost our ability to perceive reality. We end up living in a world created of duality: a duality between good and bad, rich and poor, better and worse, and this is not the reality of how things really are.

This way of thinking can have devastating consequences on our behaviour and can contribute to strengthening our *Protector*. This, in turn, makes us live life as if we are trying to prove to everyone that we are *good*, not *bad*. We try in many different ways to convince people that we are *good*. The learning association is that *good* is acceptable and *bad* is unacceptable and deserves punishment. Obviously this makes the *Protector* even stronger, as we desperately strive to be liked for being a *good* person.

We can see this when a child feels his mother loves him only if he behaves in a certain way. She is not patient with him when she thinks he is being *naughty*. As a result, the child begins to associate that behaviour as being *bad* or believe that he is no *good* whenever his mother implies that he is being naughty.

Unfortunately, some parents divide things into *good* and *bad* because they were brought up this way, too, and they pass this training on to their children, albeit with good intentions, as a way of encouraging them to get on in the world. What happens, however, is that the child begins to suppress his or her feelings, which then continues into adult life. They may suffer in silence and alone, until they are no longer aware that they are suffering at all.

From a very young age, many people learn not to express their feelings. Perhaps because they feel that no one accepts and understands them when they were hurt. They don't know that they can still be loved when they are angry, sad or needy and therefore they continue struggling to be *good* so that they will be loved. Furthermore, some even suppress their negative feelings, but these feelings remain and are triggered by events in later life. The result is that the *Protector* learns to behave very well, is extremely reliable and understanding, and therefore a *good* person.

It is fascinating to realize that the motivation to be *good* derives from fear. Based on our early learning, we are not supposed to be bad or feel bad in any way. Most of the conflicts we have in the world arise from people trying to be *good* rather than being themselves. Although this point should not be taken literally, as good people, of course, make amazing contributions in the world. Some people, however, try to be good because they are afraid to face pain, they want to avoid being bad or they are just not aware that their motivation for being good is fear, and this can be dangerous. Let us use the example of people who fight for justice or fight to protect poor people. Of course it is a good cause, but their attempt to FIGHT for this cause can also become aggressive. These reactions can be reflections of hidden aggression toward a past oppressor (mother, father or teachers, for example). The oppressor or oppression they fight can be a representation of a hidden memory of experiences of injustice they once suffered.

Another very sensitive example is in the area of forgiveness. Forgiveness is a way of relieving oneself from carrying pain. The *Oxford English Dictionary* defines forgiveness as: 'to grant free pardon and to give up all claim on account of an offence or debt.' Forgiveness is promoted by religions and social norms, and we are taught that *good people* forgive. The challenge here, however – and you can ask yourself this question – is: how many times in life did you forgive someone but deep in your heart you were still angry?

Forgiveness can be a way of concealing resentment, anger and indignation, and it can put us in the trap of trying to be good people because good people are forgiving. Yet at the same time there is still a feeling of injustice about what happened to us and that can be a suppression of aggression, which eventually leads to more aggression. I would go as far as to say that forgiveness can be used also as a *Protector's* strategy to avoid conflict because fear of conflict is a way of protecting ourselves from being hurt and we may use forgiveness as a mask of being good people.

I must emphasize here that I am not against forgiveness, which can be healing for many, but also it can be a way of protecting ourselves from reality. In terms of the relationship between the forgiver and the person forgiven, the forgiver can be the good person and the forgiven can become/

remain the bad person who has done something wrong – and we are trapped endlessly between the good and the bad.

There was a story in the newspaper titled 'I can't forgive killers; Bomb victim's mother gives up priesthood' about a vicar who admitted that she was struggling to forgive the men who murdered her daughter and so she decided to step down from her position as a parish priest.

Many religions promote forgiveness and remind us of the need for humans to practise forgiveness of one another in order to be good religious people. But you are already good; there is no need to try to be! Don't desire to heal. Don't desire to avoid pain and fear. In the desire to be perfect we end up with a never-ending desire to change what we perceive as imperfect and many complications arise within us as a result. This is an impossible and unachievable task for most people, most of the time.

Observing all your negative feelings rather than rejecting them allows you to be at peace with them. Nothing can give you more confidence than learning to observe and accept your doubts. Nothing can help you feel compassion more than observing your limitations. There is nothing more powerful for generating more love, than observing your lack of love.

I would like to emphasize again that there is no need to fight in order to change, because if we fight for peace in our lives, we are just fighting another war. As Gandhi said, 'We must never fight injustice, instead, we must strive to make it visible.'

Most of our reactions are actually failed attempts to escape from a painful reality that we can't tolerate or accept. The predicament here is that the *Protector* is a reaction to the pain of life and our reaction to the *Protector* follows the same pattern. In other words, an aspect of the *Protector* is to reject itself. This is why we need to be extremely sharp and observe the moment when we realize that we are acting from the *Protector* and outside it – with no blaming, no self-justification and no escaping. We don't want to be *bad*; we want to see ourselves as an ideal perfect person. Perfection is a belief about how we should be. The desire for a change for the better actually confirms that there is something wrong with us and then we begin to judge and punish ourselves even more. Transformation may take place if we can observe exactly who we are with warmth and compassion, without any judgement or any desires, preconceptions, ideas or opinions.

## Observe the war within

The difficulty in this journey to self-discovery arises as soon as we become aware of our protective personality, because then starts another battle in our head between judge and accused. If nothing else, realize that this clearly shows that the person who most judges you is you. The person who keeps reminding you of your past mistakes is you. This makes you separate yourself from your essence. The journey is to learn how to tolerate yourself and have mercy on yourself. If we can't tolerate who we are, we can't tolerate anyone. We need to have mercy on ourselves. We need to hold our frightened childlike self and see their fear with compassion.

Each one of us represents the world. Each one of us carries billions of cells and these cells are interacting with each other, communicating and grouping together. They are even communicating in different ways with different neurotransmitters – something akin to speaking in different languages. When we aren't kind to ourselves we often judge and criticize ourselves. We declare war on ourselves and life then becomes a battlefield of failed attempts to change. It is the same as what is happening in the world today in countries where different religious groups fight, judge and hate each other. But as we are one with our essence as individuals, so we are in the world.

We are all one, we all share one body (the Earth) and we all eat, we all sleep, we all breathe the same air. In addition, we are all born and die exactly as human cells do. Unfortunately the brain is not capable of understanding the idea that we are all one.

For example, since the 2003 invasion of Iraq, the result has been that the West has become more hated by the Muslim states than before. There are more suicide bombers than at any other time in history. The stated purpose of the war was to get rid of an aggressive dictator; there is one like that in every one of us, we hate them and the result is more hate in the world. This is an analogy for each one of us: we begin to hate ourselves if we try to change ourselves. If we fight our limitations, they will fight us back, just as it happens in the outside world. This happens as instant feedback. We are even fighting people who are fighting to stop the fighting.

We need to raise our consciousness above thinking that war is bad or even that people who are fighting a war are bad. You need to bring to mind some of the mistakes you have made in the past; bring to mind how many times you have punished yourself for making mistakes, and how many times you have regretted making them and hated yourself for making them. We think this is an effective way of dealing with them and yet we keep on doing them, which causes more pain and more mistakes, and so the cycle continues. Observe your limitations as something you have done in the past, and that is all. At the time you did not have the awareness you have now, so why punish yourself for something you did not know how to do?

Gandhi's non-violent, and extremely effective, resistance toward the British is a wonderful example of raising consciousness and he famously said, 'As long as we try to punish ourselves for our limitations, we will not find peace.'

If you treat yourself in the same way you treat the person you love most in your life, you will live with the person who loves you the most.

## Observe the moment

The journey for us now is to be still and not to attempt to change anything at all. We need to surrender to the moment of awareness and allow it to unfold to a new one, which will also change to a new moment of awareness. Every moment is an experience that is in a constant state of flux and we need to be present in the now rather than thinking about the past or future.

It takes us a lot of courage to be open-hearted to everything we see and do, and to accept our mistakes so that we no longer see them as problems. Only then will we no longer be victims of our past. The fact that you are reading this book now means that you are no longer a victim of the past memories of your *Protector*. Each moment and experience we hold on to becomes a memory we also hold on to. It is this *holding on* that keeps us from our essence, but we do have the power of changing our focus.

The *Protector* is a mechanical process and, while it does a good job of protecting us, it can overshadow our essence. This is because the *Protector* is attached to outside experiences while our essence is not.

Our essence is total awareness or consciousness, as opposed to the brain, which records every sensation, pleasurable or otherwise. Our essence functions in the *now*, as this is the only time when there is no past or future. Our *Protector* is trying to fight our reactions to our past, however, and in so doing makes our past stronger than our present. This process, in turn, constructs our future and it means we look into the future with fear and anxiety about what might happen to us. In our construction and anxiety about the future, we find ourselves no longer living in the present moment.

The *Protector* persuades us that what happened in the past will surely happen again in the future. Not only that, but we end up anticipating that it will happen as a matter of fact. Past memories and beliefs are what we know and we construct our model of the world upon them.

## Observe your suffering

Unfortunately, all of us at some point in our lives have had the painful experience of rejection or loss. Perhaps you suffered a broken heart or were betrayed by someone that you trusted. The *Protector* attempts to escape this pain by trying very hard to dismiss this person from our mind and just get on with our life. This means, however, that we make a choice to suppress pain and not to deal with it, and we can resort to showing specific behaviours like *laughing it off* or taking an *I-don't-care* attitude. In response to suffering, some people end up drinking to excess in order to *forget* or they immerse themselves more frantically in their work. Others may even end up with severe psychological symptoms.

> *'Out of suffering have emerged the strongest souls; the most massive characters are seared with scars.'*
> KHALIL GIBRAN

If we observe our pain rather than avoiding it, we may feel that a part of us is dying. This fear of losing everything can invoke our *Protector,* as it tries to fill the emptiness with many other things. If you observe the suffering consciously without trying to escape, however, you realize that it is not you that is dying but your *Protector* – the part of you that doesn't know how to love yourself, the part that is not real. Suffering puts your *Protector* under huge stress because, at the moment of your heartbreak or betrayal, your protection has failed you. The *Protector's* job is to protect so that when you suffer, the *Protector* ceases to protect you and you become the real you; you do not deny your suffering.

Suffering can be a tremendous shock, as it shakes the power of the *Protector.* The heart is not living until it has experienced pain; it is asleep until a blow awakens it. Then it gives unconditionally and each blow that penetrates the heart awakens us to sympathize with others. Our *Protector* is pretending to be strong, pretending to cope and protecting a false image. Ironically, if you reduce yourself to zero, there will be room for your essence to manifest. Our love will manifest if we are completely empty, as it is then that you will see who you really are.

*'Oh, my friend, if you are longing to be written upon, become a blank sheet.'*
RUMI

Suffering is like a fire that burns the *Protector*. What remains at the end of the fire is our essence, the real self, because our essence cannot be burned or destroyed and therefore cannot die. Our essence is the conscious present moment and nothing can happen to it. The only part of us that burns is our mask. The mask is not who we are, it is only an image, and at first we suffer if we lose it because we have become accustomed to hiding behind it to survive.

We identify with the mask as an image of ourselves. If such an image is reduced to nothing then we can see our essence. This can happen sometimes when we have a big shock in life and we feel destroyed but it is only that our mask has been taken away from us and we feel naked. Not fighting suffering can actually allow you to make contact with your essence because when we feel there is nothing left of us, it is then that the true light of ourselves shines and we become conscious of being here and now. At the time of suffering there is a lot of pain but when we recover, we are able to access other parts of ourselves that we never knew existed.

Most of us, however, try to avoid suffering because we think it is bad. This is not an invitation to promote or avoid suffering; it is about observing any present suffering and allowing it to reveal to you how your *Protector* suffers as it tries to protect you. If you do not protect or justify anything, you do not suffer. There is no suffering in the present conscious moment because all suffering is to do with the past and how we tried to protect ourselves from it. In the conscious moment the past has already passed. Having said that, do not go to the other extreme and promote suffering; this is again a trick from the *Protector* to be a victim that needs to suffer in order to heal.

Your *Protector* tries hard to make you something out of nothing. It doesn't know that being nothing is filled with love and freedom. Not being attached to anything or not wanting to be anything at all is real love. We need to experience this deep emotional layer all the way and it takes enormous courage to be *nobody* and to lose your pride. If you are willing to do that, then you are able to be free. All the emotional layers are, in fact, defences against the experience of nothingness. If you are willing to experience any emotional state deeply and completely, you will discover awareness as both the experience and as the experiencer, and then you will be free from running away from negative states toward positive ones. You will also be free from either regretting or clinging to anything. There can be no resistance to whatever emotions arise from consciousness. There will be no need to hide in stories any longer.

It takes a lot of courage to live in this world with an open heart. Our past pain makes us close our hearts in order not to get hurt and this is the *Protector's* job. If you are desperate for success, allow your heart to be broken and allow yourself to fail. If you are desperate to be with someone, then allow yourself to be lonely. Allow yourself to feel the pain if you have not allowed yourself to do so before. Allow yourself to say, 'I am not able, I am in pain, I am suffering, I am grieving and I have failed.' Then will you see what lies underneath it all.

The secret of feeling loved is the willingness to feel what it is like to be unloved and still keep our hearts open.

## Observe being unloved

So many people tell us that we must love ourselves, but how? If someone asks me if I love myself, I feel they are asking me the wrong question. There is no answer to it, because there is no method that will bring this about. We are already doing it because if we didn't love ourselves, we would not be alive today. Love may be holding your body together. If you hurt yourself physically, your body will immediately attempt to heal itself without your permission. Is this not a sign of love?

The *Protector* isn't willing to face the pain of being unloved because its main aim in life is to protect us from such feelings. This is actually the key to feeling loved, however, because if we want to be loved we must risk the feeling of being unloved first. Be willing to feel how it feels to be unloved. This is the secret gateway to the heart.

It takes a lot of loving oneself to have the courage to feel unloved and to be vulnerable – not to hide behind a survival mechanism masquerading as a loving person who is afraid of the pain of being rejected. Or perhaps hiding behind the 'saviour' and helping others, but still being afraid of abundance and the need for oneself to be saved. Again, it could be the mediator who sets aside his or her needs

DISCOVER YOUR HIDDEN MEMORY & FIND THE REAL YOU

in order to make everyone else happy. They are trying very hard to give people what they really need or to overcome their fears, which is conflict.

> *'Your task is not to seek love but merely to seek and find all the barriers within yourself that you have built against it.'*
> RUMI

## Observe how you seek love

The *Protector* is seeking rewards and wants you to be loved and liked, but the tragedy is that when people seek rewards, they become smaller than their rewards. If we relinquish rewards, we rise above them.

A direct challenge to our *Protector* is our willingness to be nothing – the pain we have carried for years defines who we are. We need to look at the uncomfortable dimensions of our personality. We need to be willing to face and meet the pain of being unloved by really looking deeply into our hearts, until we see ourselves as nothing at all. That nothingness is filled with love, as it has no attachment to anything in order to become.

The need to be loved has to be felt before the lack of fulfilment can be faced. If we can then live in this place, all our reactions will arise out of love, not fear. If we are constantly cultivating fear, we will vibrate with fear, no matter how much we try to hide it. When fear raises its head, listen to what it says. Be with fear as it is, for if you are with fear, then you are no longer in fear.

If you dare to risk losing your self-image, which you

made up from your *Protector*, you will be nothing. Only then can you find your real self.

## Observe your humanity with humility

How can we accept ourselves more? How can we find that place inside that will be patient with us when we react? How can we find a place in us that sees the world as a loving world, not a hostile one? How can we see who we are beyond love, hate and fear, and feel everything without running away or by dissecting and sorting out good from bad, happiness from sadness?

The answer can be found when we don't grab or hold on to our experiences. Happiness begins by accepting and recognizing the way we behave, rather than by blaming ourselves for what we have done.

Begin by feeling what is happening to you in every moment, even in your body. The challenge is to respect your reactions, your feelings and to begin to see that everything we have done in life is the way it was. We must understand and acknowledge that the effect of the past on us cannot be changed in any way. A moment will come into our life when we can say 'yes' to everything that has happened to us, whether hard, bad, good, boring or crazy – that is the way it was, and is. Moreover, we need to accept and say 'yes' to how we reacted to whatever happened to us. Only in doing this will we begin to leave the hidden prison of our past and no longer be victims of it, because we can now live with it. We will know when we have reached acceptance because those things that happened in the past are no longer occurring.

## Observe the unbearable

This is the way our essence experiences the world. It doesn't think what *ought* to be. When we become empty and still, watching our *Protector* without any disapproval, criticism or justification for our actions, and when we stop the search for change, then there will be a swing toward acceptance.

The journey toward healing has no destination; it is a state of acceptance, compassion, openness and willingness to be with our fears. The healing also depends on our ability to be open and accept what has happened to us even if it is unbearably painful. Thus, we will grow from being a child who could not tolerate pain and rejection, into an adult who can bear rejection without having to run away. As *adults* we will have enough room in our hearts to encompass pain and rejection, and to embrace love. Denying the unbearable is expressed in the *Protector* by attempts to avoid pain and love – and in so doing it avoids freedom.

The work you do on yourself is never finished. There is no destination, only the unfolding of possibilities and gaining of insights toward loving yourself.

# CHAPTER 4
# FEELING YOUR FEELINGS
# AS THEY ARE

*True love for ourselves allows us to embrace our pain
and fear with compassion.*

## Embrace your natural human emotions

The key to your transformation is to begin to allow your past feelings to pass naturally, but this can only happen by feeling them, not by hiding from them and allowing them to pass. There is no need for healing, learning or hiding behind any method whatsoever, but only for feeling your feelings. We need to acknowledge any difficult situation or uncomfortable event that makes us feel as if we are losing control. A normal reaction would be to get angry, feel pain and fear as we lose control of our emotions, which is too much to bear for our *Protector*. This is because of our *Protector's* need to survive; we try to regain control and correct what is happening to us in order to restore balance as soon as possible. In some cases, when the pain of the event is so intense, a remarkable coping mechanism is set in place to protect us. In children, this often happens by complete dissociation from the event.

*'Emotion is the chief source of all becoming
conscious. There can be no transformation
from darkness into light or from apathy into
movement, without emotion.'*
CARL JUNG

# Emotional detachment

We explored in Part I how emotional detachment takes place
in order to protect us from the experience of pain. You can
see this in cases where there has been a car accident, for
example. Some people sometimes don't feel the pain until
after the event. You can also see this if you watch a nature
programme where a lion catches a gazelle. The lion holds
the gazelle in its teeth and the victim becomes completely
calm and appears not to be feeling any pain but it is in a
state of dissociation from the horrific event. This commonly
happens to people who have experienced great trauma,
such as soldiers and rape victims.

After the painful event we get a chance to talk about
what happened and to process how we felt. This allows our
memory to process the situation into conscious memory
and in so doing we release our brain from storing the
experience as unfinished business or a hidden memory.
Notice how when you have had a bad day or been caught
in traffic, you talk about it afterwards until you forget about
it. The event then becomes a memory of the past. In a
healthy relationship, the person you are with should allow
you to let the event unfold from your consciousness and
listen to you without judgement. This process allows us to
agree with the past and to let it stay in the past. In cases

of more serious trauma, this can also be achieved through counselling or therapy.

Painful feelings are locked up in the hidden memory box of our consciousness. This *box* may need to be opened again, albeit with a lot of care and love to enable it to happen. If we don't have the courage to do this, then sometimes life will give us a shock in order to open the box. When this happens, many people will run away from the pain and simply find another box in which to store the painful memories. Examples of a new *box* could be a new relationship, career or a house move; these are replacements to suppress the pain again.

If we are physically injured in any way, our system rushes to heal the wound, using the amazing natural mechanisms of cell growth, called the epidermal growth factor. In the same way, when we are emotionally hurt our conditioned, forces of repression keep us calm and safe to save us from feeling pain and to ensure our survival. Unfortunately, the pain is already activated and is trying to connect with our consciousness in order to be able to heal while at the same time we fight to *box it up* again. This can naturally cause a huge conflict in our consciousness – the attempts to heal as a solution become a problem of running away from pain and can result in an interminable merry-go-round, which causes greater pain.

This can be observed when, for instance, we want to get close to someone and experience love, but at the same time we fear the thought of loss and of being abandoned in the future. The result can be that we might retreat from love without wanting to, even sabotaging the relationship before it has started. Inevitably, this behaviour will only serve to reinforce the original pain of wanting to be loved and get close, before running away.

As young children, we didn't have a choice in making sense of our experiences. We took them into our system and had no option other than to protect ourselves with a survival strategy, in order to avoid a pain we could not understand.

Each time the *Protector* prevents us from dealing with a challenging or stressful situation, our hidden memories remain in our unconscious present and are not processed. So these reactions are still running round in circles and it requires an extraordinary transformation to be able to see what is happening within us at each moment.

## The human consciousness strives to complete the incomplete

For healing to occur, we need to make our hidden (unconscious) memory available and to link our emotions with the original experience, which caused them in the first place. The hidden memory is stored as body response patterns and is released by external stimuli. With the help of education and hypnotherapy, it is possible to make our hidden memory consciously accessible so that the brain can understand and make sense of things in the present time.

Resolving unresolved states is the key to our healing. If we manage to consciously make sense of what happened to us in the past by feeling it once again and learning about what happened, while feeling safe at the same time, then we can release the brain from the compulsive suppression of unremembered feelings to complete our unfinished business.

An analogy would be to think about all the books you have read and, in particular, the one you haven't finished reading yet, where you have yet to complete the last chapter. You are more likely to remember the book you haven't finished than the ones you have completed. Think of incompletion as something you started but didn't finish and you will know that you are more likely to remember this. Alternatively, think of a relationship that ended abruptly, without any chance for goodbyes; it will be more likely that you will think about this relationship and go over and over it in your mind in order to make sense of the *why*, than if the relationship had ended and the ends had been tied off together properly. It is the same with memory.

The brain will always go back to its original wiring. Even now, as I am writing this book, if I write a sentence that doesn't make sense, I have to go back and correct it. If I don't do this, I am more likely to feel that something isn't quite right. Conversely, if you read a page in this book and don't understand it, you may not move on until you have made sense of it. Unfinished business needs to be finished.

As you are, right now, think of a time in your life when something was left incomplete and you will realize that it keeps coming back to your mind over and over again.

The human consciousness is about completions and your consciousness will strive to redress anything that is incomplete. This is why patterns in life keep being repeated: they are attempts at completion and, thus, healing.

Therefore if the brain doesn't make sense of a painful experience in our past, our fear reactions will keep repeating themselves and pushing us toward the same feeling again and onward, in order to find completion.

The key word here is *feeling*. If we didn't feel the painful experience and haven't made sense of what happened, we would be forbidding ourselves to feel pain. Unfortunately, we end up hurting more, not less. It is easy to walk away and run from pain, but it only brings deeper pain as a result.

## Embrace pain with compassion and mercy

See and feel your pain with the eyes of compassion, but not with any sense of duty to make it better and not to feel. Only compassion can unravel the deep pain we have carried alone for years. Our compassion has the ability to melt the pain into just a feeling. As our body needs food, we need love and physical touch and care. Love is the connection that is missed by our disrupted connections with the people who should have loved us. Lack of love has become pain. We can make the connection again when we look at our pain with love. Most of our suffering comes out of a lack of love. Successful therapists can feel their clients' need for love.

Compassion helps us to stop running away and to begin to free our trapped and unexpressed feelings. It is all about making connections again by linking our physical sensations to our perceptions of the world, to our deep emotions of fear and then, finally, to our *Protector's* impulses. In other words, we need to bring to conscious awareness the defences we use to avoid pain or fear. Accepting the defences we use, such as humour, aggression and holding back, will allow us not to run away and to find completion.

Our brains can tell us where we hurt in any part of the

body but can't feel pain itself. The brain doesn't feel pain and so, if we live in avoidance of pain, we might develop illnesses that will force us to wake up to the pain anyway. We need to let the pain *be* instead of blocking it because if we don't embrace it, it will continue, perhaps even to the next generation. To conquer fear is to feel the pain, but as long as we avoid our pain, fear will remain.

Unless we embrace the suffering of the past, it will continue. We don't realize how trapped we are in our invisible prison by a prison guard called our *Protector*. Put simply, we must follow our feelings and never withdraw from life. We need to use our pain and suffering because these are the very things that make us conscious human beings. We see that children cry spontaneously in response to hurt because it is natural and healing; maybe we need to have a good cry, too. Some of us, however, have suppressed our feelings to the point of never crying. Have the compassion to meet your pain and to embrace suffering, to bear the unbearable and to touch your pain with love.

It takes a lot of loving oneself to have the courage to feel the pain and to be vulnerable – not to hide behind a survival mechanism. But the more we try to get rid of the fear and the pain, the more we follow teachings, gurus, therapy and achieve intellectual ideas. The more we try to escape, the more we will turn our fear into suffering.

What we really don't realize is that it isn't the pain that is repressed but our reactions to our overwhelming past feelings. We can also see that our reaction to pain is like our reactions to most things, which cause pain in our lives. Often, when we approach a problem, we try to find the solution in our mind, but we don't try to find out how our mind relates to the problem.

## To heal is to feel

Healing begins when you get in touch with the sensations that precede your usual reactions. Because the *Protector's* role is to suppress pain, feeling it again allows the trapped reactions, which could not be released at the time, to be released. In this process we can also be aware of the *Protector* coming to stop the pain by distracting you by or doing something else in order to avoid feeling the pain. Healing yourself is all about making connections again by linking your physical sensations and perceptions of the world to your deep emotions of fear and, finally, to your *Protector's* impulses. In other words, we need to bring to consciousness the *defences* we use to avoid painful experiences or fear. Because the role of the protective response (defence) is to keep the pain repressed, we need to see beyond these *defences* in order to express our buried feelings. We need to begin to open the secret gates to our hearts. When fear arises, it is an attachment to joy as much as an attachment to suffering. It is the same thing as aversion is to negative attachments. Fear is not the problem but our identification of the fear. The more you investigate your fear, the less you will be beholden to it.

*Knowing about hidden memories allows us the opportunity to see ourselves from the person of the past to the person we are today.*

We can travel back in time to see the wounded child and allow ourselves to relive the experience, which affected us so deeply, so that we can start to make sense of it. Loving ourselves will allow us to go through the fear of the experience from the perspective of our present looking at the past, so that we feel the past experience, but without fear. We need to understand what our child-self must have felt when it didn't know what love was.

Having mercy on ourselves means opening our hearts and making space to contain our pain. We will be able to see better out of this openness, as our heart will allow us to embrace every situation as it is. We will become like a parent who, on seeing the faults in their child, contains and affirms them without punishment or judgement.

If we manage to acknowledge our pain without sorrow, we will be open to connect the truth of our past to our present feelings without having to enact a story or drama in order to avoid criticism and without worrying that people will not like us. It is much easier to make a connection between our painful experiences in the past and our resulting behaviour if we are present and conscious of living in the *now*. We can then begin to accept the way we react to contradict our intentions.

> *'The greatest challenge to increasing self-awareness*
> *is to remember the difference between unconscious*
> *reflexes and conscious consciousness.'*
> PETER D. OUSPENSKY (1878–1947), RUSSIAN PHILOSOPHER

The majority of our limitations stem from our memory connections with events that happened very early in life. At this stage of our lives we were unaware that we were learning, as we were not able to convert this learning into early memory. Our early reactions to danger were purely childlike in order to face difficult experiences. We did not understand the danger in the way that an adult does and, because of this, when we react as an adult with a child-like protection, we need to be patient and have mercy on ourselves, because we learned this when we were children.

Now we are learning something new and we must not punish ourselves when we repeat an old pattern. You can understand this better if you think about what it is like to watch a child learning to walk. They will fall many times before they can stand and take their first steps, but they don't punish themselves when they fall. Therefore, be willing to be like a child when you try to heal protective strategies that do not serve you – after all, you learned your protection strategies when you were a child.

*'Pain is inevitable, but misery is optional.'*
Tim Hansel (1941–2009), *You Gotta Keep Dancin'*

It takes a lot of strength and commitment, and it is not easy to face oneself with humility. Paradoxically, such willingness not to run away from ourselves is the ultimate authority we can possess over our lives. Such authority can never be achieved by force – only by humility.

Don't look at your fears and your pain; just keep looking at yourself with deep compassion. This way, you will be able to embrace your humanity and be conscious of your essence, provided you don't stand against the suffering, which comes from hiding from it. If you don't do this, you will only reinforce the reality of suffering until that moment arrives when you can embrace your suffering with compassion. Then you will be free.

## Thinking your feelings or feeling your thinking

*What we know, we do not feel.*

I talked about awareness earlier and it is important this kind of awareness doesn't require any effort. Effort means struggle to change, but there is no need to change anything. The first step is purely to bring about awareness and observe what you see. One of the aspects of the *Protector* is the need for transformation but there is no need to transform or to become enlightened or healed. Change cannot come about by force or intellectual ideas; it emerges through insight into every moment.

Change can't happen by thinking alone, because we are dealing with deep emotional memories, physical sensations and feelings, together with false perceptions. Our emotions are the key, as they are our only method of interacting in a world of relationships and are what makes us human. By thinking alone, we might lose touch with the reality of those emotions and sensations, and replace our needs with ideas, but this can be another aspect of our *Protector*, which allows us to hide our feelings by talking about them.

Our intellect will attempt to label our feelings as anger, love or disgust and so forth, but no amount of intellectual analysis will reveal the depth of our feelings issuing from past unresolved painful experiences. Intellectual conclusions can be an escape from reality. To change emotions, we need to be able to touch our emotions, to express our emotions, not to think about our emotions.

The way we escape is by naming our feelings, for instance by saying, 'I am depressed.' Immediately we have labelled the feeling. The term 'depression' was invented by the Western world and imported to the East when pharmaceutical companies wanted to expand. Observe what you do when you have any feelings. Most of us immediately name the feeling as 'love', 'anger', 'pleasure', 'hate', etc., but this naming is an intellectual process, which prevents us from seeing reality and cuts us off from our feelings. In other words, the 'name' comes between reality and us.

The intellect tries to give a name to what happened to us in the past and, as a result, we lose the ability to feel the feelings. If we give feelings a name, then we will have to find a name to change our feelings. We try to label how we feel about ourselves and to rationalize our actions in words, but words are never the same as that which they represent. The word 'love' is not love. The word 'surrender' is not surrender. The word 'acceptance' is not acceptance. Words are merely attempts to feed an intellect that is hungry for understanding.

Many of us spend our lives training our intellect in order to find peace. We think that intelligence makes us better able to deal with our limitations. By doing exactly that, however, we are more likely to block our emotions instead. The intellect doesn't have the ability to feel, so we spend our lives in training to connect with true feelings but not actually feeling.

The intellect divides life into such things as 'if I make money I will have a happier life' or 'if I meditate I will find peace' and 'if I pray then I will be a good person'. But again, these are mere words without emotions. They are in fact symbols that represent, rather than those which are.

We need to surrender to the complexities of life. If we empty our minds from projecting patterns onto the world, we will make a space to allow insight to come to us that will reveal the mechanism of our *Protector* in each moment. This means observing each moment as a precious opportunity to rise above your limitations. If we try to be in harmony with our feelings, then they will distance themselves from us.

So the journey between the intellect and feelings we have felt in our earlier experiences is the bridge that we need to cross to reach the unresolved painful experiences, as opposed to constantly repeating our reactions to that experience. It is only then that we will begin to make sense of what has happened to us in the past and leave the prison of the hidden unconscious memories. We can then open a new world of self-exploration and see the act that we present to the world as being a mask. We will then see the fear behind that mask, the pain behind the fear and then finally our essence will emerge by itself. We don't need to seek it out; it has been there all along.

We do, however, need to appreciate our intellect because without it, you would not be reading this book, which in turn will help you to appreciate your essence, which is beyond intellect.

# CHAPTER 5
# NOTHING TO FEAR

*Pain and fear are the* Protector *unmasked.*

## Step toward your fears

Don't be afraid of your pain, anger and fear. Fear has a right to be in your heart, as it is a natural human reaction. When we relate to our fear with compassion, we release an enormous caring and love for ourselves. When fear comes, we need to look into it and ask ourselves what exactly it is we are afraid of. Are we afraid of losing our home, our family, reputation, character, money or health? Can we allow fear to come closer to our heart and allow it to stay without being denied? Are we willing to permit it to remain there and see what it is?

The trouble is that we have been encouraged to take our awareness away from our fear, so let us turn everything around. When you notice your resistance to fear, remind yourself to take a step closer to it.

If we look very carefully into fear we will find that we are not afraid of anyone, but we may be afraid of pain, which is, in fact, psychological pain derived from many past experiences. Because we don't want to disturb the pain, then the fear remains present. Our *Protector* ensures we don't disturb our fears and painful feelings, but the dilemma here is that the real pain can't hurt you any longer, because it was created in your past and no longer actually exists in your present.

If we are afraid, we can't become aware. Looking fear in the face requires real focus and energy, which is often dissipated with words and conclusions. We spend our lives in the service of fear and every decision we make in life is based upon it, even our hope. Fear is the urge to seek what we miss and we never look at what is underneath our fear because we spend our energy in getting rid of it, suppressing and denying it.

Awareness creates a willingness to stop such un-successful attempts and enjoins us to see it and own our fears. This will, in turn, bring about a realization that can take us beyond fear and pain to a place that is untouched by the past, and into self-realization and the present moment. Saying, 'I must be free of this fear' engenders more of it, while saying, 'I will look this fear in the face' brings transformation.

Although, be aware that the *Protector* has another trick up its sleeve when we say, 'Yes, I will face my fear.' When we simply talk about it or read a book about facing our fears, rather than actually feeling them, then this is another kind of suppression, using theories to find the cause. The mind, which is afraid of suffering, can't eliminate fear but is capable of finding other ways to escape from the task and therefore will still be enslaved by fear. Fear is the product of the past and it continues through verbalization, symbols and images into our present. Analyzing fear gives it more life and thus we risk ending up in a circle of being afraid of the fear of being afraid of what we think we fear!

Fear will always find something to be afraid of, but it is not the object of the fear which is the problem; it is the subject. If we are afraid, we will then act on it and create more of it, but if we go toward it and face it, we may find it is no longer there. The courageous walk toward their fear, instead of running away from it. If we practise doing this, a moment will come in our lives when we no longer act to get rid of pain and suffering, and it is only then that we shall see beyond it because we realize that our essence has never been touched by it. From this point, we can learn so much about our true selves and begin to find our essence. This approach to fear brings courage to the mind and allows it to rest there in mercy instead of in resistance or by escaping from reality.

*'Courage is fear running in the right direction.'*
PATRICK WHITE (1912–90), AUSTRALIAN NOVELIST

## Fear is an attempt to use fantasy to change reality

If we open up to our fear we can still feel afraid but without feeling the need to escape and without even the need to affirm how afraid we are. We simply experience the fear itself as it is. I am not speaking of physical fear, as fight-or-flight responses are natural and appropriate to the human organism; I am speaking of psychological fear. When we meet our psychological fear then it reveals deeper emotions. Treat your pain for what it is and you will find a way to search no longer for the whys and wherefores of it. Freedom will come by itself once you make a commitment to yourself to be free.

We are afraid of our fear and of losing control. The more we are peaceful, still and calm toward our limitations, the more we will be able to hear our essence and handle any external conditions. The way to live from our essence is through the willingness to deny nothing and to have the courage to face the reality that perhaps we were not loved enough as children or suffered unpleasant experiences at an age that meant we could not really understand them. Perhaps we only got praised for our achievements instead of who we were. Then we can begin to understand how later on in life we made many sacrifices in order to achieve love. Some people work hard to try to achieve the sensation of being loved: some try too hard by being too kind, some try to achieve love by making many compromises and some even by hurting themselves.

These sacrifices were the unsuccessful attempts of our *Protector* to seek love by working hard to achieve the impossible. It helps us to realize this is a transformation in itself and we can then begin to start living from our essence and feel loved for who we are. This way we will realize the extent of our strategies and that *we can't have enough of what we don't really need*. We will also stop seeking because we are emptied of struggle and when we no longer struggle to earn love, we will be loved.

*'When you are sorrowful look again into your heart and you shall see that in truth you are weeping for that which has been your delight.'*
KHALIL GIBRAN

## Objecting to pain is suffering

To overcome our resistance to pain, we need to make a journey to get back to our early unfelt feelings. The resistance, which is the foundation of the *Protector*, causes mental suffering, which suppresses the pain even further. This automatic protective reaction to survive the pain is so immediate that we are not able to feel or make any sense of our feelings. In our unconscious attempts to run away from pain, we mysteriously become tied to what we hate and fear. This is an energy that attracts situations similar to the very thing we are trying to avoid or of which we are afraid. Consequently, we will be exposed to similar painful experiences in various other forms and to repeating the same reaction of suppression, serving only to emphasize our pain and suffering.

From the brain's point of view, the resistance is in our thoughts, which are stored in our hidden memories, and they also create energy through our interactions with our environment and relationships. This vibration of energy matches other vibrations of similar forces, so we don't attract what we wish to attract; we attract that which we think about, and that which we want to avoid because they are stronger in our thoughts. We are the makers of our reality, even the reality that does not serve us.

> *'Fear arises when there is avoidance of the fact,*
> *a flight; then the very escape itself is fear.'*
> JIDDU KRISHNAMURTI (1895–1986), WRITER AND PHILOSOPHER

Most of the activity of the *Protector* is conditioned to expel, deny or numb grief and pain, because they are so difficult to face. We have to be very sharp and watchful of how skilful the *Protector* is in avoiding pain. We need to recognize and explore whatever arises and not run away. To reiterate, running away only reinforces something that actually only existed in the past. We are conditioned to chase positive emotions and run away from negative ones. Running away from negativity enforces it and brings more of it. Running away uses the same strategy we used to protect ourselves in the past. Unfortunately, this desire enforces the power of the *Protector* and so long as the hurts are unfelt, the fear will remain. One of the masterful ways we use is to talk about our pain or about how the past caused us pain, but without feeling anything. Ironically, talking about pain is just another *Protector's* strategy to avoid it. In this way we attempt to solve the wrong problems, and the wrong problems have no solutions because we are not in tune with the issue; we are caught up in running and avoiding.

We have been trained to pull away from anger, pain and fear, before we get a chance to feel them.

## Embrace the writer, actor, director and producer of your life story

Telling a story will also make us attempt to escape from new painful experiences in order to distract ourselves from dealing with the accompanying unpleasant feelings. For example, sometimes, perhaps in discussion with another person, we begin to feel uncomfortable and expect to be rejected without knowing why. This is because all these processes for dealing with our fear are working away subliminally beneath our awareness. We may not know that the reason we are feeling edgy is because our senses are overshadowed by a perceived danger – a danger for which we are already primed. We need to link the priming experience of the mental model – the emotions, perceptions, behaviours and, most importantly, our physical sensations – and feel. We can start to heal when we get in touch with the sensations that precede our usual reaction to fear.

All these are the clusters of hidden memory linked together. Our story and our sense of self are made up and maintained by both hidden (unconscious) and remembered (conscious) memory merged together, but they are not who we are; they are memories, which we make into a false reality.

The way we think about our personality is not real, because it is only the idea or image we have about ourselves. In turn, these ideas and images influence what we feel and think about ourselves, and how we perceive the way in which other people feel and think of what our family and friends have told us. The images we have of ourselves are not who we are. Instead, these perceptions support the story we have regarding who we think we are; we don't really have a life, we have a story about our lives and the story is not real. Observe your story; it will become a process of realization that there is, in fact, no story. Maybe only then will we have a life.

> *'No one can make you feel inferior*
> *without your consent.'*
> ELEANOR ROOSEVELT (1884–1962),
> FIRST LADY OF THE UNITED STATES 1933–45

We need to acknowledge that our *Protector's* hidden defences and reactions to past experiences have many

DISCOVER YOUR HIDDEN MEMORY & FIND THE REAL YOU

different forms and expressions, just like actors in a play. This play, however, is the play of life itself. Some of the parts are like a comedy, while others are akin to a tragedy, but they all feel almost real. During the acts we aren't aware of our reactions. Not only that, but we go further and are in complete denial of the consequences of our reactions and the results that they produce in the external world, because we are not aware of doing it while we are doing it.

It takes a huge amount of love for oneself and others to acknowledge and appreciate that denial is part of, or a step toward, healing. If we judge people for their denial, it becomes our denial, too. Our protections are like an act written by a hidden author, directed by a hidden director and manifested by a hidden producer who puts all the parts together in a play called *life*. We need to appreciate that the child within us quite innocently made up a way to live in an adult world, as they perceived adults living in a bigger drama. They invented this drama, bringing it into their play in order to live.

For example, when I was very young I used to spend hours playing with small toy cars and soldiers while making up stories about them and how they could survive. I made up many characters, which all responded and interacted with each other. Many children do this, of course. This was my way of occupying my time to avoid feeling alone, which was caused by the lack of contact with my parents and other people. What I didn't realize was that these characters I had created and I were rehearsing for the many roles I would play in later life. All this play-acting was my naive childlike reaction to surviving the fear of being unloved and uncared for by my family. It was a fantasy world involving many people interacting and compensated for the actual lack of interaction around me. I was writing a script for my part that I had constructed in my mind. When I grew older, inevitably the world, relationships, careers and situations have reflected back to me the careful script I planned long ago. I chose careers that involved social change, therapy and getting many people together so they did not become lonely, too. The hidden memories of my reactions to loneliness led to constant activity and a busy life to make up for a world of isolation in the best way I knew how.

The power of our protection can also produce successes, too – if we are conscious of how our limitations can also bring success – and so why would we curse our past and the gift it brings to us now, no matter how hard it was? The past is a gift if you embrace your journey.

But if understanding and acceptance of the plays we have devised, as a reaction to our early lives, is so crucial, how can I therefore bring about change without trying to change as another level of protection?

The answer to this lies in the magical power of observation. Observation can have powerful effects. Research has shown that the act of observing can alter the observed. It is possible for us to change our experience of reality merely with deep observations. In fact, observing deep pain and hurt with love will change pain and fear into loving.

By observing my daily interactions with others and my choices in life, all of the above has been revealed to me by cultivating a deep love for myself and honouring my journey in this life. Deep reflection and observation teach us how to feel and appreciate what it is like to be human – a human with all its imperfections.

Do not seek perfection or desire perfection; just see your life now with deep compassion for others and for yourself.

Desiring perfection can be yet another role we play, but the role of the *good* person is only an act. Open your heart and embrace humanity with patience and compassion for the adult and the child you once were.

The *Essence* process is seeing how your life unfolds by choosing compassion for yourself and other people in your past. The work on ourselves is supported by having mercy for all the reactions and strategies that resulted from the many attempts to find solutions to cure painful intolerable experiences, which have resulted in unsuccessful solutions that you made as an adult. All the painful compromises you made, the ways you sometimes settled for less and, of course, then received less; the way sometimes you gave up your happiness for others in order to get their love. These are aspects of the *Protector*. In fact, such choices were good choices in helping us to survive at that time, and our *Protector* was created in order to support and enable us to feel the love to which we were entitled but perhaps did not get. Even now the *Protector* still tries to provide us with childish solutions in order to get love and avoid the danger of lack of love.

> *'The unexamined life is not worth living.'*
> SOCRATES (*c*.469 BC–399 BC), GREEK PHILOSOPHER

In the process of discovering our hidden memories and finding the real us we started by reflecting on our childhood attempts to relieve ourselves from the pain and the conflicts we saw in our family. We need to examine all of these attempts that kept us occupied for a long time, as some of us repeatedly played these roles with baffling accuracy in a drama that we could never control. Many of us are swept away by the storms of relationships where we find ourselves needing to be alone yet at the same time so desperate to be with someone and to be loved. For some of us the actor in us has managed to continue playing the act of being alone with so many people around on the stage. Even when the play is over and the audience has gone home, many people do not even realize that they are safe, because the loyal professional actor cannot stop acting the well-rehearsed script in the hidden play of life.

*'All the world's a stage, and all the men and women merely players.'*
WILLIAM SHAKESPEARE (1564–1616), *AS YOU LIKE IT*

The journey toward our essence begins by total acceptance of ourselves as we are, exactly as we are. This acceptance includes observing and embracing the actor in us, as we would with any professional actor in the theatre. The big challenge is to work on ourselves in such a way as to finally see that the actor within us *can still be safe without the act*.

*'Everything changes once we identify with being the witness to the story, instead of the actor in it.'*
RAM DASS

Witness the *Protector's* role with loving. You can only see this by being watchful of all your reactions that are expressed in the desperate desire to be loved in order to avoid pain. It is a very challenging journey simply to watch ourselves and see how we react to the world, life, people and situations as *witnesses* and not as *fixers*.

*Real freedom can come from surrender out of courage, not rebelliousness out of fear.*

**Exercise for the reader**

*Close your eyes.*

*Go back in time and think of a painful situation in the past.*

*Recall what happened.*

*How long ago did this situation occur?*

*How old were you?*

*Try to remember as much as you can about everyone involved.*

*Pause.*

*Reflect deeply on the effects those experiences had on you, without judgement or running away.*

*Scan your body and feel any pain in any part of your body that holds a memory of this past.*

*Notice any fears you have carried from the past.*

*What conclusions or decisions did you make about yourself as a result of this situation?*

*Did you think that there was something wrong with you?*

*Did you think that you were unlovable?*

*What assumptions did you make about yourself?*

*What impact did your conclusions and assumptions have on your life today?*

## Making sense of your world

In doing this exercise and reflecting on the experiences that created your *Protector*, do not make sense of your limitations by rationalizing your actions and using words to represent past painful realities. Life is an experience but ideas can't stop feelings as they suppress our instinctive responses. If you say, 'I found the way,' this may mean that you have lost the way to healing.

Transformation is possible only from the known to the unknown, not the other way around. Not knowing anything is being present in the moment. Surrendering your knowing about the cause doesn't change your behaviour. Be willing to take the consequences without knowing what they will be. Move from your heart, and take the consequences.

Greatness does not always come when things are going well, but it does come when you are tested with disappointments and sadness. Only if you have been in the deepest valley can you ever know how magnificent it is to be on the highest mountain.

## Choiceless awareness

We need to allow our conscious to live with what happened to us in the past. You can do this by paying attention to your fears and anxieties instead of avoiding them. I want to say to myself I am afraid or anxious, not with judgement, but with curiosity, until I become conscious of my unconscious fear and begin to understand exactly what I am afraid of, and why. From this place, we can then begin to transfer unconscious past experiences to memory, where we will begin to consciously describe what happened to us from our hearts, our feelings and our insights, and not from methods or intellectual ideas. You don't need any method to be able to do this. Just notice your fear and anxiety, which will then signal your original feelings. At this moment it is important to be still and quiet and not react by killing the messenger. Keeping quiet and still, just observing what is being revealed to you.

Be open to drifting into the most unlikely places within the dark waters of your unconscious, where the hidden difficult experiences are locked away. Maybe these memories are not so dark after all. Allow yourself to reflect deeply on the effects that those experiences had on you, without judgement or running away, and make as many connections as possible. These connections and insights will help you develop a sense of the memories.

Insights can't be written or spoken but must gently unfold as you are guided by the understanding of how your life has been affected by your hidden and painful experiences. These insights are all we need to understand our lives, and only we can do this for ourselves. It is only when we understand ourselves that we find the truth and thus free ourselves from the past and go beyond the old movement of time into the new. Our brains can understand and be conscious of every single one of our deep feelings. The unconscious parts of us can't be changed by force, but we can become aware and consciously sensitive of them.

Once we live from awareness, we will make our lives work, as we won't need to be told how, or to learn anything else in order to heal. We will be free.

## Stillness

We must be very careful here not to try to be still. If we try, we are not. If we observe our lack of stillness, however, we will naturally become still. When you are still, you get in touch with your essence with the conscious mind that is inside you. We need to search more deeply into ourselves and to follow our thoughts so that we can trace their effects on us and on others. By carefully experiencing each experience of our lives, we will learn about ourselves. When we are intent on discovering the whole process of our life and our reactions to it, then every incident and each reaction become a means of discovery, of knowing oneself. This patient watchfulness can then become very little effort.

The way to control anything is by doing less. If you have water in a container and the water is moving and you want it to be still, it is best to leave it alone and just observe it. Your quiet observation will be reflected in the water. However, if you interfere and try to force calmness you will make it move even more. Like water in constant movement, the *Protector* is very good at adapting to a volatile world, inconsistencies and people in order to survive. The best way to become aware is to observe the *Protector* without interference.

With stillness and quietness in your head, you will be able to observe your internal conversations and also the way you react to life and what part you play in it. If people react to you or treat you in a certain way, we can then observe how your *Protector* reacts to them at the same time you are doing it and then you can make an alternative choice.

> *'Learn to watch your drama unfold while at the same time knowing you are more than your drama.'*
> RAM DASS

Let us start by allowing a witness within ourselves. Let us choose to watch the show instead of acting in it. Observe the drama, as it plays out, and witness the pain and fear – any pain of rejection or loneliness. Notice it as it is, as if you were being observed, but without feeling separated from yourself. You will notice that what is being played out is a translation of the way you see life. This will bring about extraordinary self-knowledge without any effort on your part; only then will you be free. Provided there is fear and anxiety about what happened in the past and what might happen next, however, we will find that self-love and freedom are elusive.

> *'Knowing is not enough, we must apply.*
> *Willing is not enough, we must do.'*
> JOHANN WOLFGANG VON GOETHE (1749–1832),
> GERMAN WRITER AND POLYMATH

# CHAPTER 6
# LET NEW EXPERIENCES
# INTO YOUR LIFE

*Life experiences have lasting effects on us only by*
*being stored as memory in the shape of connections in*
*the brain.*

## The essence process

The essence process works in two dimensions: one is an
experiential process that allows people to engage in real-
life situations which elicit real-life reactions (our protective
behaviour) and can also uncover past hidden memories. In
this way we begin a process to learn that it is possible to feel
safe in a threatening situation, unlike in the past, when we
did not feel safe. This can also be done by guided imagery
techniques, which allow participants to revisit past difficult
events in a dissociated way while remaining physically
calm. These non-threatening experiences transform the
memory patterns to bring them to an end. The courses are
conducted in an extremely safe and loving environment,
which helps to facilitate a process of allowing people *to let*
*go* of all their defences and be real. This takes place in an

environment with constant interaction with many people to reflect on day-to-day life.

The second dimension is that learning experiences are provided that can lead to changes in neurological connections. People are also able to discover which strategies support them and which don't. In order to be more effective, we need to know the ones that do not support us and add new ones that really do work by practising new experiences. Because the programmes in our brains were built by past experiences, we must acquire new experiences to create new supportive programmes.

These new experiences create fresh programmes. If we practise and repeat these often enough, they will eventually override the old, unsuccessful programmes in our subconscious.

*Experience is beyond the power of words.*

We have explored the first dimension by way of the experiential process. Now let me talk about the learning experience that can lead to changes in our neurological connections. I will use here a very simple and powerful metaphor. There is a lot of emphasis on breathing in mediation and in most Eastern traditions, which provides us with an amazing tool for transformation.

We can only breathe in after we pause, and then breathe out. We cannot breathe out and in at the same time without this pause. This is a very apt metaphor for how we can be free. Every time we take a breath it is an opportunity to allow us to experience receiving and giving, and letting be.

# Experience receiving and giving and letting everything be

When we breathe in we *let in* air to support our lives. This is allowing. The moment between the *in* breath and *out* breath we *let be*. This is being. Then we breathe out and *let go*. It is as if by giving up life first *(letting go)* and pausing, we let life *in* again. The next cycle is the pause again between the *in* breath and the *out* breath. This small pause is empty. We do the same when we walk, learn, take risks or try new things; we let go of what we know and trust, and wait, and so allow new things to come into our lives.

> *Letting everything go, letting everything be,*
> *letting everything in is the secret of living a*
> *rich and inspired life.*

The word *let* is one of the most useful words and has the key to making positive changes in our lives. It has many dimensions, such as 'let be', 'let go' and 'let in'. Let these three instructions guide you in creating new experiences and, consequently, new beliefs and new behaviours, resulting in a new reality which matches your intentions. Let me start at the beginning.

Let the truth of the past into your heart with all the accompanying painful experiences. They have always been there but without your conscious consent, so don't kill the pain. If you get a headache doing this, you must realize that a headache doesn't include an inbuilt painkiller and it doesn't mean your brain is lacking aspirin. The brain is experiencing deep emotional feelings that need to be *let in* to your consciousness and felt. If someone hurt you, let the pain in. Let the experience of it in and this will allow you to *let in* the understanding of how to *be* (let be) and then to *let go* of the pain. It is a natural process of the body to feel and let the feelings be, and then let the feelings go. These feelings need be felt and acknowledged, allowed to exist and allowed to leave and heal, just in the same way that we breathe.

## Let in

Change your experience by taking risks and ask for anything you want to receive. Let in what you want to receive by asking for it. If you ask, there is a 50 per cent chance you will get it but if you don't, there is 100 per cent chance that you won't. By receiving you experience more of allowing yourself to be loved.

Consider that every breath you take is a reminder of how it feels to receive. Think of the time someone gave you something and part of you didn't want to receive it. This is akin to depriving yourself of breathing in, and of life itself.

As babies we were entirely dependent upon other people for our survival and we received from them 24 hours a day. In that first experience we were given to, 100 per cent. As we grew, we began to learn to be independent and we learned to stop receiving. Receiving begins with our parents but it is not just about receiving material things. The foundation of receiving is emotional and as a child grows, they need to have parental support to assist their understanding of the experiences they are having. They need support to learn how to manage their feelings and explanations for their experiences. If children don't get this kind of feedback they can't make sense of what happens to them and they will respond in the same way as their parents responded because this is the only method they can see. If this support is omitted, they will try to survive the best way they can to keep themselves alive, and this is where the *Protector* comes in.

Some people become very independent and they refuse to receive anything – money, emotional support, or even love. The attitude here is 'If I don't fend for myself, then I am a failure'. In order for this to heal, change your experience by becoming interdependent and allow people to support you even if it feels unnatural. The most effective people have an amazing talent for allowing people to support them while at the same time retaining their independence. Change your experience by letting in support and accepting gifts, money and love from people. This experience will change your beliefs and you will not need the *Protector* any more.

Let in the image of what you want in your life. Nothing is created outside you before first being created inside you. Begin to allow yourself to see what you would like to be in your life, visualize what you want to see and let these images flow into your consciousness. Many of us imagine failure, not success, and so we allow in what we don't want.

Let nature do everything for you and get everything to cooperate with you. The highest form of knowledge is not to know how, but *know-how*.

Let in the feelings that you have what you ask for and you *will* have it. Act as if you have already got it.

*Gratitude allows you to receive what you already have.*

Let in what you already have; begin to allow yourself to receive all the things you already have by being grateful for them. As you read this book now, there will be many people in the world who don't have the luxury of reading a book and they may not have had the chance to learn to read. They may not have a warm place to sit or a roof over their heads. Look around you and see how many things you already have and let yourself be grateful for them.

As you read this book now, there is a percentage of the population in Cairo who live in graveyards, including children who are brought up in graveyards alongside dead people. When I lived there, I saw children sitting on the pavements studying for exams under the streetlights. Some of these kids go to universities and become very successful later in life. I have also observed when I worked in the British National Health Service, many children refusing to go to school and being sent for counselling.

## Exercise for the reader

*You can do this with your eyes closed.*

- *Bring to mind all the people you have helped and supported, and allow them to thank you for what you have done.*

- *Bring to mind all the people with whom you had relationships and thank them for the good things they have done for you.*

- *Bring to mind your mother and thank her for giving you life and other things she gave you over the years.*

- *Bring to mind your father and thank him for giving you life and other things he gave you over the years.*

- *Bring to mind the closest people in your life – members of your family or friends – and thank them for all the things they have done for you.*

- *Bring to mind all the material things you have and thank yourself for creating them.*

When we appreciate all the good things we have in our lives, we actually allow ourselves to receive *without paying back*; this is the *Protector's* strategy.

One of the problems we have, particularly in the West, is that many children have come to expect things to be given to them and are slowly learning not to be grateful for what they have. If we aren't grateful, we may never let in the rest of what we can have in our lives.

Let supportive relationships into your life. The fear of rejection can be healed through the experience of a loving relationship, although it may take some time, but an unloving relationship can reinforce the original feelings of rejection.

## Let be

Let the past be. Embrace the past and don't deny anything whatsoever from it. It is what happened to you and that is a fact. Denying your past will lead you to fighting the facts, but as I have mentioned before, fighting the past means we constantly live in danger, as if in a war. We will not be at peace if we constantly run from pain and chase happiness.

*'Stop leaving and you will arrive. Stop searching and you will see. Stop running away and you will be found.'*
Lao Tzu, sixth-century bc mystic philosopher
and author of *Tao Te Ching*

This is the moment to pause and be empty and be full. This is the moment to see everyone who hurt you and let him or her be. If you let everyone be, they will also let you *be* because you will not think about them any more. Our enemies have a hold on us because we are busy wanting to punish them. We can resent them all day and nothing will happen to them, only to us as we continue living in pain and resentment. These feelings can block our energy and impede us from creating what we want. Letting be is an experience of freedom. Resenting people is a desire to seek justice with aggression. This means we have not been able to let the past be. Letting everything be is an experience of expansion and it is a measure of your greatness. It is an experience of peace and humility.

If you let people be with peace, they will let you be with peace, too. Letting be must start with letting our parents be. Letting everything be is one of the highest forms of wisdom; it is a surrender, but with power. If we can allow things to be as they are and agree with what happened to us in the past, we can move the past to the past and complete unresolved situations. The past hidden memories will then stop controlling our actions. Putting the past where it belongs is central to finding your essence. We can't do this while we are hanging on to situations from the past and trying to change them according to what the solution should be. This also includes our image of ourselves. The challenge is to let ourselves be exactly as we are, with no blame or regrets. When we let our limitations be as they are and let everyone else's limitations be as they are, then we are in harmony with life itself.

Many people are still hanging on to a sense of miscarried justice at what happened to them when they were very young and go as far as seeking compensation.

Ask yourself, who do you want to punish? And why?

Let everything you are hanging on to be, especially punishing people for what happened to you. Let what happened between your parents and you in the past *be*. The time has to come in our lives when we should no longer use people and our parents as the reason for our failures.

Allow yourself to grow by seeing how your *Protector* was created, and how it allowed and promoted situations. You deserve to be free from the limitations you have put upon yourself.

You must be very careful here, for in order to achieve this you must not ignore the pain and hurt, the anger and fear. The above will only be achieved once you have allowed all these feelings to come and go, otherwise you will be in denial, pretending that you are spiritual and that you are perfectly capable of forgiving everyone and everything.

## Exercise for the reader

- *Close your eyes and recall all the people in your life who have hurt you or challenged you.*

- *Talk to them one at a time. As you see them before you just say to each one: 'I let you be as you are, and in doing so I let that part of me that is like you heal.'*

- *Take a deep breath in and then exhale.*

- *Each time you talk to any of these people let those who hurt you be as they are – there is no need to send hate or wish them pain or even to feel love.*

- *Be totally empty.*

- *Be completely surrendered to your emptiness.*

- *Let yourself be with negative judgements about yourself.*

- *Let the world be to do what it wants through you.*

- *Let everything in your life be as it is.*

- *Let yourself be as you are.*

- *Let everything be as it is.*

- *Let your past be as it was.*

- *Let your past decisions be as they were.*

- *Let the world be as it is.*

The very willingness to let the fear *be* means we are not trying to change. This is healing. Letting your fear be means you are being directly in touch with your fear and pain as they unfold within you and this requires a lot of courage.

*'The way to do is to be.'*
LAO TZU

# Let go

If something is not working in our lives, like a relationship, work, a project or a friendship and this situation is becoming a burden or causing us a lot of stress, then these are signals that it is not really what we want; we just think we want it because we are afraid to let go. Life will always support us to get what we want and not what we *think* we want. Do not be afraid to let go of anything in your life.

> *'Some of us think holding on makes us strong, but sometimes it is letting go.'*
> HERMAN HESSE (1877–1962), GERMAN-BORN SWISS POET,
> NOVELIST AND PAINTER

We don't *let go* because we are afraid of loss; we are afraid of something going away from us. Here again, these are hidden memories from the past that are coming into our present and influencing our lives. Unfortunately, if we don't *let go*, we aren't free to get something new. If there are other people involved then we are holding them prisoners with us, too. If the situation results in them leaving, then we may experience the very thing that we don't want. This is another aspect of our *Protector*, who doesn't want us to experience rejection by keeping people in our lives that we actually don't need any more.

We need to *let go* in the knowledge that the universe will always provide us with what we need the moment we allow a space inside ourselves for something else to come.

If you can accept who you are and believe that nothing in you needs to be made perfect, better or stronger, you will experience a whole new way of living. Therefore, accepting the past means *letting be and letting go* of it.

Sometimes we find it difficult to *let go* of something because we can't accept something new. The reason for this is that we have invested so much time and energy into our model of reality. If we don't accept our past, however, we will be controlled by what we can't accept. If we are intent on change, the way to do it is not to focus on the 'I must change, I must change' because if we do that, we will only entrench ourselves even deeper. We need to accept not just our circumstances and what brought them about, but the pain and fears that are attached to them.

Your *Protector* may not accept you but you can accept it as it is and transformation comes at the very moment of accepting what happened in the past without the desire to change it. This means we need to agree to life *as it is* and *as it was*. The reasons we did not agree to life *as it is* was because when we suffered painful experiences as young children, it was not possible to agree to something painful. We simply didn't understand. For some, the pain is too much to bear and acceptance of it will seem impossible but they will not be able to let go of anything they cannot accept, or understand the injustice of.

> *'A man is rich in proportion to the number of things he can afford to let alone.'*
> HENRY DAVID THOREAU (1817–62),
> AMERICAN AUTHOR AND POET

How much time do you spend trying to keep what doesn't belong to you any more? We must never be afraid to *let go* of anything. Everything we possess now in our lives will one day not be ours any more.

## Let go of past relationships

This is one of the hardest things for some people to do. If you are willing to take the risk, look at anything you have kept from a previous relationship, such as photos, letters and gifts, and give them away. If you don't, there will be no room for another relationship in your life.

## Let go of people

Who is in your life at the moment that is not serving you and their company brings you down? They are good people too, but not necessarily the people you need around you to support you and uplift you, so don't be afraid of letting them go. Otherwise, you will find that you want them around because you need to be needed. Let go of your desire to punish people for what they have done to you or to someone else.

## Let go of holding on to money

Give money away and you will experience that you have more.

## Let go of objects

Let go of all the objects in your home you really don't need any more and which you have carted around with you from house move to house move. You will then begin to experience that you deserve new things. If you don't clear out the old, the new cannot come into your life.

If you have clothes you never wear any more, give them away. Again, you will experience that you deserve a new wardrobe and with the old wardrobe cleared away, there will be room for the new.

**Let go of the false image that your *Protector* is trying to keep**

Let go of worrying about other people's opinion of you.

Let go of wanting to be right all the time.

Let go of measuring your worth by your achievements.

Let go of seeking love.

Let go of comparing yourself to anyone.

Let go of pleasing people.

Let go of suffering.

Let go of your desire to change the world.

# Letting in, letting be and letting go

So it is clear that if our beliefs, assumptions and reactions are based on experience, then we need to change our experiences in order to change our reactions.

Letting in, letting be and letting go will create new experiences opposite to the programmed beliefs and decisions that you made about yourself. They will override the beliefs that undermine you, as they are the result of a memory that has, thus far, limited your life. They are, in short, feelings of experiences in unconscious memory, which are constantly repeating themselves. They can be overruled by new experiences and new memories.

# CHAPTER 7
# HEALING IS A PROCESS
# NOT A METHOD

*Our* Protector *is a lens through which we see our reality. And when we look at the world through our protective character, our vision is altered or distorted.*

Our protective character sees the world through hidden memories and beliefs. This is, in effect, a false personality, which is attached to the events of the past and its dynamic is more apparent in relationships than in anything else. The *Protector* has functioned, adapted and shaped itself in successive relationships and in disparate attempts to balance out the inconsistencies in our environment. It is like putty and can constantly change and modify. Most of our conflicts in relationships and the world in general arise from our *Protector's* distorted perception of reality.

We interact with what we see in the world through our *Protector*; it is the mask behind which we hide. The mask filters our reality according to our perceptions and how our original conditioning and experiences have made us.

Our interpretation of the world is based upon assumptions and beliefs, and we don't know whether or not they actually exist in reality. Because we fail to recognize their power, we are hindered by our *Protector's* reactions. In other words, we can be hijacked at any time and when this happens, we live unconsciously, not consciously.

## Transformation begins

Our journey begins by grasping the idea that our *Protector* represents our limitations. Then we can begin to realize that it is possible to transform our lives and how we see the world. Indeed, we have a responsibility to do so if we wish to live from our true essence – in other words, consciously, in the moment and not in the past.

Our *Protector* anticipates what will happen to us in the future (based on our assumptions about the past) and can therefore repeatedly sabotage our efforts to be effective in every relationship and interaction.

It creates our model of reality and our map with which to navigate through life. The more we map our reality, the safer we feel. It is as if an invisible fortress protects us. Life for some people has become like living in a fortress, always anticipating disaster and pain.

## But where is the enemy? Who is the enemy? What is it?

The enemy is the past that still lives in the present through our *Protector*. Living in this way means that life itself has become a constant state of siege. Having said that, we must also acknowledge our *Protector* with kindness and understanding because it is only trying to help us survive in this world. Its choices were good ones at the time when we had no others, but now we are no longer in danger and the war is over. We have no need for further protections or a fortress. Our *Protector* is too aware of pain and therefore conjures up ingenious ways of avoiding pain and fear in order to protect us from further pain and disappointments. It does this before we even have a chance to process or choose from a neutral position. It predicts what will happen to us and also predicts the behaviour of other people toward us. For instance, if you have an argument with someone, you will find you already know how you are going to respond even before you have heard what the other person has to say. In this scenario we can end up regretting our reactions even while part of us does not admit that we have made a mistake.

We need to look deeper at how these beliefs became lodged in our brains in the first place and how they control us and manifest in our everyday encounters with others. We need also to look at how these beliefs and memories interact with and shape our lives, and produce behaviours that often contradict our intentions.

We have started a journey to understand the relationship between our awareness, our experiences and how the human brain is organized, and how we try to react consistently from the past in an inconsistent world in the present. The differences between our model of reality and the real world are divided and filtered by our *Protector*.

Many teachings tell us to live in the present moment and not to live in the past. We need to go back into the past, however, to go back to the time when the parts of our brain that organize memory were not fully functional. The wounds from our early years are still open and raw because the brain didn't have the ability to understand or process them at that time. We constantly pattern our experiences in order to make sense of what happened to us. In other words, we are constantly looking for conclusions and connections so we can make sense of the things that we can't understand. We therefore form patterns of connecting situations in order to feel safe because we know what is happening to us. Yet the mind does not have to rely on any set patterns or any conclusions. We often look for consistencies in order to feel safe, by seeing the past and looking for patterns. We need to free ourselves from creating and inventing patterns.

## Understanding our forces of energy

The brain acts as an instrument for receiving, storing and communicating what is shared between all of us. There is constant interaction in every experience, and we are surrounded by the mental world of others, just as we are surrounded by the physical world. Most of our reactions and thinking is shaped by whomever we are interacting with, and this is how we experience ourselves in relationship to others.

The constant interactions between all of us create forces of energy. These forces are derived from all our communications and are constantly being encoded in our brain. The people who are most important in our lives have the greatest impact on us and can also have an effect on our environment. Our *Protector's* constant interpretation of the world also allows us to participate in creating an information field in the world, which we share with everyone. This shared energy is not localized in the human brain. The brain receives signals from everyone around us, interprets them and produces a model. You can observe this when you travel to other countries by the similar way in which people live and interact with each other. This is because they are in an energy field made up of all the forces of interactions, beliefs and assumptions. This is why it is impossible to change a culture from the outside.

Our *Protector* reacts to our deep feelings from the past and we try to think ourselves into ways we can be happier and more effective. But we cannot think our way into feelings. We have to feel the feelings. Sensations allow us to access sensations, and each level of awareness (feelings, thoughts, senses) contributes toward its own connection. Therefore when we re-experience the feelings associated with a person or event with our new awareness in the present moment, we realize we are safe now. This is how healing can take place and we can live with past painful experiences and bring closure. To do this we need to reflect deeply on our lives in order to make sense of difficult childhood experiences and past events, which is something we are unable to do when we are very young. We will then be able to utilize our mature intellect to access the time before our brain was fully developed and reach these unresolved emotions. It won't happen through words or explanations, as we can't access pre-verbal experiences in this way. Our task is to use our intellect not in an analytical way based on our previous presumptions and theories, but purely in order to make sense of how all these presumptions and theories have influenced our present. With deep loving and neutrality, it is possible to put the past to rest and let the past be old and not new at every moment in the present.

We must not be afraid of travelling back into our past in a conscious way (with the support of our intellect), because we have already relived these past experiences many times for most of our lives in an unconscious way. The only way to get to something is through it, not around it. Thus, we can take control of our past instead of allowing the past to control us. To do this we need to keep our minds very sharp and be able to reflect without the distraction of our protective character's reactions. This will allow us to connect to our essence, the now, which is beyond all limitations.

## Our essence, our true self, is here now

Our essence is not attached to anything; it is everyone and does not even need love, because it is love itself. We often try very hard to get love or to be loved. Our *Protector* fools us into thinking that we must seek here and there for it, and use all sorts of strategies in order to bring love into our lives. However, these strategies are often unsuccessful. If we want love, all we need to do is to connect to our essence. To be with what is in the *now*. Our essence is inside us, so we don't need to run around looking for love outside. Because the *Protector's* aim is to avoid pain, it looks for love and comfort, and consequently struggles, fights and manipulates to obtain love. We are missing the fact that love is already there within us, in our essence. Only our essence is able to witness the unfolding of our life drama and challenges without reacting.

Love is so vast it can encompass and tolerate anything. To prove this, remember a time when you loved and felt loved deeply by someone. You loved them no matter what they did because you were in your essence in the now and nothing else mattered, but the moment when you started to feel insecure and unloved, you started to judge everything about them and react to past relationships and your own past rejections, bringing these into your current relationship.

All we need do is observe our reaction to what people have done to us in the past, and witness all these events without judging anyone or yourself and without wishing that things could have been different. Wishing things to be different means you are trying to bring past belief into the now. Be with everything as it is; be with yourself as you are because our essence is who we are and our *Protector* separates us from that. We lose our true self when the person with whom we are interacting shapes our reactions and thinking. This is how we experience ourselves; we think this is who we are. This is the final illusion created by our protective character. The *Protector's* thirst to ensure our survival takes us away from the present and makes us live as if we were still in the past.

## Compassion is awakened, not forced or learned

Our brain may not be capable of conceiving the idea that we are all one, not separate individuals. In the moment, in our essence, we are all one. It takes a shift in consciousness to actually grasp that this is a process of our lives when we transcend all our judgements, comparisons, past experiences, what people did to us and live with compassion for our journey and all the people around us in this world.

Look at the people around you with compassion and ask yourself, who is inside them making them alive? At the same time ask yourself, who divided these people from me? The answer is: your brain, your beliefs, religion and your culture.

We need to be willing to be nothing, without any image at all. Self-surrender is the price of real freedom and it is a price that is absolutely worth paying. There is a paradox here, and that is that if a person loses himself, he will also lose his protector. Only then will he actually find himself. Our essence was not born and therefore will not die. It is every one of us at the same time and, by constant observation and compassion for our journey and others, we can find that place that contains the whole world. Because the *Protector* is motivated by fear, it will pick up on our fear of separation. Thus, we will be afraid of loss, death or anything that we feel will separate us from others. This is hard to grasp, especially when we see turmoil, aggression and injustice in the world, but if we are willing to look very deeply, we will find that all the aggression and injustice are also as much a part of us as love is.

# EPILOGUE

*The* Protector *is part of the process of our awakening.*

## A journey without a destination

Our past and our childhood memories are revealed in every aspect of our lives; they are almost written on our faces and expressed in our voice and actions. We can see that all our beliefs derive from our early life and were influenced by the relationship we had with our parents and by the collective energy field of the people among whom we lived. We have learned through generations of conditioning how to survive. We unconsciously define who we are by our reactions and interactions in relationships. We have developed a character that we think we are. We have lived in this conditioned protective character – our *Protector* – as if in a trance. The journey now is to use our *Protector* as a vehicle of our awakening.

Our *Protector* was important in order for us to survive and to protect us from re-occurrences of past painful experiences or the fear of being unloved or unwelcome. As we get older, however, we gain in wisdom and see the world in a different way. The future hasn't yet arrived and we don't know how we will feel when it does. The final journey is all about the present moment. No moment is the same as the one before. Our life is connected to the past like a river and, as famously posited by the Greek philosopher Heroclitus, 'We cannot step in the same river twice; its waters have already passed us by.' All events in our lives have already passed and they keep on moving. You are not in the same moment as when you started reading this book, or even this sentence.

Our brains want to hold on to the past and it creates patterns of reactions (as in our *Protector*) with a strong desire to continue our reactions to a past that no longer exists. The brain is programmed to do this in order to protect us from future events that will duplicate what has happened before. It is very tempting to go back into the past because we don't know who we are without it. We identify with our past and we cannot stand being empty, or being nothing, so we become a bunch of memories that don't move with the flow of life.

Let the movement of life take you, as it flows like a river reaching the ocean, to your destiny. Observe it as if you were yourself a leaf from a tree floating downstream. If life grabs you with its challenges and you end up being swept away, then follow the flow of the river – don't try to swim against the current. The river will take you to the right destination. All suffering comes from our inability to allow life to flow.

Ask for what you want, then allow life to provide it. It will support you in getting what you really want – not what you think you want.

We cannot stop the movement of life and we cannot stop ourselves from growing old. We cannot stop the days, the nights, the mornings or the evenings. These events are not separate from each other; they are only movements, like the movement of the river flowing into the sea.

In the same way, if you look at a human cell you will see that it is constantly changing. It starts with a cell splitting into two, then four and eventually it expands through the biological movement of the universe and there is nothing to stop it. We can try to swim against the current and avoid the unavoidable, objecting to what is happening or what people have done to us. Or we can be in agreement with the direction and flow of the river of life and also accept where everyone else wants to be and let them be. In this way, we allow the river of life to carry us. The power of the river is the power of our destiny in life. We can then also connect to the power behind our destiny, which is the biggest mystery of this life, just like the vast ocean.

The questions to ask are, can I be empty with a quiet mind and keep an open heart even in the most difficult moments in my life? Can I stay in a state of unconditional observation of everything that has happened to me? Watching life going by like a river includes observing how my *Protector* operates and limits me. Can I see how my *Protector* is attached to the past and how it tries to do the same things as before? How it lives in the reactions of the past according to how things were, not according to how things are moving now? If I am in this state long enough I may see a light that never flickers through fear, pain or worries about survival.

Within everyone there is a light that is concealed by pain and fear experiences. The time has come to embrace painful experiences, not run away from them; these are the crucial steps toward awakening our essence. It is important to see our own light rather than that of others, because our essence is our realization that does not need any teachings or methods.

This journey is not about fighting or learning to get to your essence and it is not a preparation for the time when you can be free, enlightened or spiritual. When the moment comes when we can accept everything, everyone will love even those things which are repulsive, bad, boring or crazy and see them as *the way things are*, while at the same time saying 'yes' to our past, no matter how painful it was, from a place of acceptance (not from a desire to be spiritual or the desire to be good). This is how our essence experiences everything.

Our essence doesn't agree or disagree with anything that has happened to us in our life. It doesn't hold on to any beliefs or conclusions about who we are. If we live with a quiet mind and an open heart we can let everything emerge as it is. Only then will we stop trying to play the game for everyone. We will find the real person who is image-less and all our reactions will be borne out of love, not fear. If we react out of fear, then we will be constantly cultivating more of it and we will show fear no matter how much we try to hide it. Our consciousness will emanate fear in the form of the protective character.

This book has now come to an end and my wish is for you to be able to embody what has unfolded herein, which is to be able to arrive at a deep understanding of your journey through life, and also to understand the journey of your parents and the journey of the whole of humanity. To be able to have the courage to stand alone with humility, with a quiet mind and open heart; to face your journey with compassion for everything, as it is, with everyone, as they are, and in every moment and in each situation of your life.

Whenever we meet people, we need to remember that our essence is the moment of silence before we react; this moment is the real action. In this way, we will see that we have a choice to bring something different to our lives and the lives of the people around us. The choice is between being completely empty of any conclusions, ideas, beliefs or judgements and having an open heart, or remaining bound to our *Protector's* expectations and beliefs.

> *'The mind of the perfect man looks like a mirror –*
> *something that does not lean forward or backward in*
> *its response to the world. It responds to the world but*
> *conceals nothing of its own. Therefore, it is able to deal*
> *with the world without suffering pain.'*
> SUN TZU, SIXTH-CENTURY BC CHINESE GENERAL
> AND AUTHOR OF *THE ART OF WAR*

There is no need to pretend to be spiritual or wise; wisdom does not appear because we seek it or have read about it in a book. Instead, wisdom grows out of the many challenges that we face in life. It emerges from how we have endured in the past and surrendered through strength, not weakness. It emerges from the way we face the reality of our past and take our stance, taking a neutral position between right and wrong. Seeking spirituality is an illusion in order to avoid taking responsibility for our day-to-day lives.

There is no one situation or challenge in life of which we need to be free, apart from ourselves. We are prison and prisoner. Once we understand this, we are free. It is very hard for the mechanical *Protector*, which is designed to react, to be able to grasp that we are all one and our essence is one. The way we function in the world depends entirely upon where we stand and whether we are against or for someone or somebody, but if we are not standing anywhere on either opinions or assumptions, then we do not need to have any position at all in order to arrive at any conclusions.

*When we bow to reality, wisdom will emerge from*
*the challenges we have faced in life. We will face the*
*consequences of our actions with love.*

The whole mystery of the universe is in each one of us, as it is constantly unfolding itself through the expression of our reflective being, where everything we see is a projected image of who we are. The mystery of the universe vibrates in everything we say and do. If we look into the mirror of reality, we will see that where we are now is the destination of our journey so far. We are as large or as small as we think we are, and in order to make our dreams come true, we must remember who we are at every moment. When we stay true to ourselves, we will see our deepest dreams projected in the universe. There is no distance to travel, as we are the journey and the destination.

If we live from our essence as our centre, we will no longer be reactive in a mechanical way to life situations and only then will the journey no longer be about ideas and how to apply them in our lives; it will be about how to accept and integrate all aspects of ourselves with deep compassion.

Finding ways to heal our past and our hidden memories and transform our lives to freedom, finding ways to live from our essence as our centre: living this way will support us not to be reactive in a mechanical, pre-programmed way to life situations. Only then will the journey no longer be about ideas and how to apply them in our lives; it will be about how to accept and integrate all of our aspects with deep compassion.

# Last words

In every moment of our lives, in every interaction with every person, our essence is awakened by awareness and compassion, not forced by knowledge and preparations.

# FURTHER READING
# AND RESOURCES

Berlin, Heather A. and Koch, Christof, *Defense Mechanisms: Neuroscience Meets Psychoanalysis, Scientific American Mind*, April 2009

Chamberlain, David B., *The Mind of Your Newborn Baby*, North Atlantic Books, 1998

Kalin, Ned H., *The Neurobiology of Fear, The Hidden Mind, Scientific American Mind*, special edition 2002

LeDoux, Joseph E., *Emotion, Memory and the Brain, The Hidden Mind, Scientific American Mind*, special edition 2002

Interview with Peter Levine, by Victor Yalom and Marie-Helene Yalom, 2010; www.psychotherapy.net/interview/Interview_Peter_Levine

Mukerjee, Madhusree, *Hidden Scars: Sexual and Other Abuse May Alter a Brain Region, Scientific American Mind*, October 1995

Parker, Randall, *Brain Scans Show Rejection Causes Pain Similar to Physical Pain, Biological Mind*, 14 October 2003; www.futurepundit.com/archives/001708.html

Penfield, Wilder, *The Mystery of the Mind: A Critical Study of Consciousness and the Brain*, Princeton University Press, 1975

Verny, Thomas and Kelly, John, *The Secret Life of the Unborn Child*, Sphere Books Ltd, 1982

# THE ESSENCE PROCESS

Our heart is the first thing that is formed when we are in the womb. This is our centre, where our ESSENCE resides. Approximately three months before we are born we begin to become CONSCIOUS responsive beings. Our first response to a safe or an unsafe world absorbs and reflects the environment inside our mother. If our mother experiences negativity then this is our first introduction to the world as an unsafe environment. This elicits our earliest response to experiences of PAIN. We cannot make sense of pain at this stage, we can only feel it.

In the early years after we are born this pain response may grow stronger if our environment in the outside world also feels unsafe, if we feel unloved or have difficult experiences we cannot make sense of. FEAR is a natural reactive layer that is formed to protect us from these painful feelings. A protective reactive behaviour (the PROTECTOR) it is often formed to protect us from feeling the fear and to suppress the pain. The stronger the experience of pain, the stronger the fear and the stronger the protective reaction. All these layers are trapping our essence and hiding who we really are.

Transformation begins with awareness and compassion for ourselves, enabling us to uncover our essence and to learn to live from the heart and not from pain and fear. Our essence is our consciousness now. Living in our essence means living consciously. Our essence is highly creative, evolving and moving with life to create and live our dreams and aspirations without unconscious limitations.

# ABOUT THE AUTHOR

**Dr Menis Yousry** was born and grew up in Cairo. He worked for 15 years as a Family & Systemic Psychotherapist and Psychologist in the National Health Service in the UK. He established the Essence Foundation in 2003, through which he delivers experiential personal development courses worldwide.

His academic research and professional experiences of working with people in many countries led him to develop the Essence Process, which crosses all cultures, genders, religions, beliefs and nationalities. It is a unique approach for moving beyond theory and methods, enabling participants to discover the hidden memories from their early years that stimulate their subconscious negative patterns. He connects the highly *individualistic* influences of Western therapeutic models of family systemic ideas with the philosophy and wisdom of Eastern *group* culture. Such themes informed his earlier career when he founded the first Arab Family Therapeutic Service in the National Health Service in order to practise mixing Eastern and Western ideas to work with people from many cultures. This was the subject of his first book, *Understanding Arab Men: Towards More Effective Systemic Family Therapy.*

www.essence-foundation.com